I0813733

What Depth of Love

Devotions on the Cross and Resurrection

CHARLES H. SPURGEON

EDITED BY GEOFFREY CHANG

New Growth Press, Greensboro, NC 27401
newgrowthpress.com

Cover Design: Faceout Studio, faceoutstudio.com
Interior typeset and ebook: Diane King, dkingdesigner.com

ISBN: 978-1-64507-570-7 (hardback)
ISBN: 978-1-64507-571-4 (ebook)

Library of Congress Cataloging-in-Publication Data

Names: Spurgeon, C. H. (Charles Haddon), 1834-1892 author | Chang, Geoffrey editor
Title: What depth of love : devotions on the cross and resurrection / by Charles H. Spurgeon ; edited by Geoffrey Chang.
Description: Greensboro, NC : New Growth Press, [2025] | Series: Old made new
Identifiers: LCCN 2025021721 (print) | LCCN 2025021722 (ebook) | ISBN 9781645075707 hardback | ISBN 9781645075714 ebook
Subjects: LCSH: Jesus Christ--Crucifixion--Sermons | Jesus Christ--Resurrection--Sermons | Baptists--Prayers and devotions | Devotional calendars--Baptists | LCGFT: Sermons | Devotional literature | Prayers
Classification: LCC BT450 .S683 2025 (print) | LCC BT450 (ebook) | DDC 232.96--dc23/eng/20250916
LC record available at https://lccn.loc.gov/2025021721
LC ebook record available at https://lccn.loc.gov/2025021722

Printed in Colombia

29 28 27 26 25 1 2 3 4 5

To Jubilee, Ransom, and Addison

Contents

Introduction

This devotional contains readings from Spurgeon's sermons preached throughout his ministry, following the passion narrative of Christ and culminating in the resurrection. From Gethsemane to Golgotha to the empty grave, these sermons proclaim Christ crucified and risen, the blazing center of Spurgeon's theology and ministry. But rather than moving quickly through this familiar narrative, these forty readings will allow the reader to slow down and meditate on this familiar account, focusing on the fascinating details of Christ's final moments on earth: Why did he wash his disciples' feet? Why was he crowned with thorns? Why was he silent before Herod? Why did the heavens grow dark? Why was the stone rolled away? What can we learn from his resurrection?

There are forty readings, so you can use this resource in the forty days of Lent leading up to Easter Sunday and beyond to help you meditate on the cross and the resurrection. But Spurgeon would say not to worry too much about the church calendar but make it your ambition to repent and meditate on Christ crucified all year round.

> Do not let anybody come in, and tell you that it is necessary for your salvation that you should abstain from this meat or that drink, that there is a merit in fasting for forty days in Lent, or that you

> cannot be saved without observing such and such a holy day. Your salvation is in Christ. Keep you to that, and add nothing to this one foundation which is once for all laid in him.[1]

In every sermon, Spurgeon's goal was to point his hearers to that gospel in all its realness. There really was a Jesus of Nazareth, truly God and truly man. He was sent by God the Father. He lived a perfect life of love and righteousness, and he offered that life as a substitutionary sacrifice for sinners, bearing the wrath of God in their place. And through that death, Christ conquered death. Jesus rose from the dead bodily, physically, as a sign that his sacrifice was accomplished and accepted by the Father. He ascended to heaven where he sits right now at the Father's right hand as our faithful High Priest. Now, through faith in Christ, sinners can be forgiven, reconciled to God, and one day, raised in resurrection life like their Savior. Apart from the incarnate, crucified, risen, and reigning Jesus Christ, there is no good news. As the apostle Paul says, "If Christ has not been raised, your faith is futile and you are still in your sins" (1 Corinthians 15:17).

But beyond presenting these historical realities and doctrinal teachings, Spurgeon's other goal was to present the gospel "ever fresh and ever new."[2] Every sermon was

---

1. C. H. Spurgeon, *The Metropolitan Tabernacle Pulpit: Sermons Preached and Revised by C. H. Spurgeon.* Vol. 39. (London: Passmore & Alabaster, 1893), 120.

2. C. H. Spurgeon, *The Sword and the Trowel; A Record of Combat with Sin & Labour for the Lord.* 1875, (London: Passmore & Alabaster, 1875), 4.

an opportunity for Spurgeon to turn the diamond of the gospel and show a new facet of the glory of God in all its brilliance and beauty. For Christians who have heard the gospel before and who think they have seen all there is to see about Christ, Spurgeon invites you to come once more to the Scriptures, to the diamond of the gospel, and marvel afresh at the love of God shown in the cross and resurrection of Jesus Christ.

Finally, these sermons not only presented but also defended the truth. Spurgeon preached these sermons during a time when a "new theology" was on the rise. This teaching took the language of the Bible but reinterpreted it through a rationalistic worldview, questioning the historic Christian doctrines of the church about the person of Christ, the atonement, and the resurrection. But in these sermons, Spurgeon armed his people from Scripture to attack false teachings and defend the church with the truth. So don't be surprised to encounter some hefty theological reflection in these sermons. After all, the good news of Christianity rests not on sentiment but on doctrinal truths of salvation. Preaching in 1887, Spurgeon described his defense of orthodox Christianity like this:

> Dear friends, I am going to preach to you again upon the cornerstone of the gospel. How many times will this make, I wonder? The doctrine of Christ crucified is always with me. As the Roman sentinel in Pompeii stood to his post even when the city was destroyed, so do I stand to the truth of the atonement though the church is being buried beneath the boiling mud-showers of modern heresy. Everything else can wait, but

> this one truth must be proclaimed with a voice of thunder. Others may preach as they will, but as for this pulpit, it shall always resound with the substitution of Christ. "God forbid that I should glory save in the cross of our Lord Jesus Christ." Some may continually preach Christ as an example, and others may perpetually discourse upon his coming to glory; we also preach both of these, but mainly we preach Christ *crucified*, to the Jews a stumbling block, and to the Greeks foolishness; but to them that are saved Christ the power of God, and the wisdom of God.[3]

Spurgeon was not unique in his fight for the truth of the gospel. In every age, Christians have had "to contend for the truth that was once for all delivered to the saints" (Jude v. 3). We too have errors to combat in our day.

But Spurgeon's example is a helpful reminder of how we hold fast to the truth of the gospel. Yes, we must rightly hold fast to the right doctrines, or as Paul instructs Timothy, "follow the pattern of the sound words that you have heard from me, in the faith and love that are in Christ Jesus" (2 Timothy 1:13). But even more, we must embrace these truths through an ever-deepening faith, appreciating more and more the treasure that we have received in the person and work of Jesus Christ. Christ must be more to us than a doctrine to be defended. He must be a living Savior to be cherished and embraced.

3. C. H. Spurgeon, *The Metropolitan Tabernacle Pulpit: Sermons Preached and Revised by C. H. Spurgeon.* Vol. 33. (London: Passmore & Alabaster, 1887), 374.

Only those who love Christ will be equipped to proclaim him. Only those who delight in the gospel will be able to defend it. Spurgeon's resolute commitment to the gospel flowed from his joy in the gospel, his only hope in life and death. May this little devotional then equip you to defend the truth of the gospel in our generation by strengthening you in the knowledge and joy of Jesus our Savior and helping you to savor the glorious implications of the resurrection.

Geoffrey Chang
Kansas City, MO
January 1, 2025

Day 1
The Blood of the Covenant

"This is my blood of the covenant, which is poured out for many for the forgiveness of sins."
Matthew 26:28

Remember that in the sacred supper, you have the bread as a separate emblem of the body, and then the wine as a separate symbol of the blood; thus you have a clear picture of death, since the blood is separated from the flesh. "As often as you eat this bread and drink this cup, you proclaim the Lord's death until he comes" (1 Corinthians 11:26). Both acts are essential.

Upon the death of Christ you are invited to fix your attention, and upon that only. In the suffering of our Lord unto death we see the boundless stretch of his love. "Greater love has no one than this, that someone lay down his life for his friends" (John 15:13). Jesus could not be more loving to us than to yield himself unto death, even the death of the cross. O my Lord, in your bloody sweat, and in the piercing of your hands, and feet, and side, I see the highest proof of your love! Here I see that Jesus "loved me and gave himself for me" (Galatians 2:20). Beloved, I beg you to consider often and lovingly the sufferings of your Redeemer, unto the pouring out of his heart's blood. Go with him to Gethsemane, and thence to the house of Caiaphas and Annas, and then to Pilate's hall and Herod's place of mockery! Behold your Lord beneath the cruel scourges, and in the hands of the executioners upon the hill of shame. Forget not one of the sorrows which were mingled in the bitter cup of his crucifixion—its pain, its mockery, its shame. It was a death reserved for slaves and felons. To make its deep abysses absolutely bottomless, he was forsaken even of his God. Let the darkness of "*Eloi, Eloi, lema sabachthani*" (Mark 15:34), bear down upon your spirit till, as "you sink in awe, you also rise in love." He loved you better than he loved himself! The cup means love, even to the shedding of his blood for you.

Our blessed Savior would have us hold his death in great reverence: it is to be our chief memory. Both the emblems of the Lord's Supper set forth the Savior's death. This peculiarly Christian ordinance teaches nothing if it does not teach this. Christ's death for men is the great doctrine of the church. We profess ourselves partakers of the merit of his death when we come to this table; our Lord's death is then remembered, shown, declared, testified, and trusted in. Evidently the Lord Jesus means us to treat the fact of his death as a truth to be made preeminently prominent: he would not have instituted an ordinance specially to remind us of the shedding of his blood, if he had not regarded it as the forefront of his whole earthly career.

The other ordinance of our holy faith also sets forth our Lord's death. Are we not "Buried with him by baptism into death?" (Romans 6:4 KJV). Is not baptism an emblem of his being immersed beneath the waves of sorrow and death? Baptism shows us that participation in Christ's suffering by which we begin to live; the Lord's Supper shows us that participation in Christ's suffering by which that life is sustained. Both institutions point to his death.

Besides, beloved, we know from Holy Scripture that this doctrine of the death of Christ is the very core of Christianity. Leave out the cross, and you have killed the religion of Jesus. Atonement by the blood of Jesus is not an arm of Christian truth; it is the heart of it. Even as the Lord said of the animal, "the life of the flesh is in the blood" (Leviticus 17:11), so is it true of the gospel, the sacrificial death of Jesus is the vital point of our profession. I know nothing of Christianity without the blood of Christ. No teaching is healthy which throws the cross into the background.

The other day, when I was inquiring about the welfare of a certain congregation, my informant told me that there had been few additions to the church, although the minister was a man of ability and industry. Furthermore, he let me see the reason for failure, for he added, "I have attended there for several years, and during all that time I do not remember hearing a sermon upon the sacrifice of Christ. The atonement is not denied, but it is left out." If this be so, what is to become of our churches? If the light of the atonement is put under a bushel, the darkness will be dense. In omitting the cross you have cut the tendon Achilles of the church: it cannot move, nor even stand, when this is gone. Holy work falls to the ground; it faints and dies when the blood of Jesus is taken away. The cross must be put in the front more than ever by the faithful, because so many are unfaithful. Let us endeavor to make amends for the dishonor done to our divine Master by those who deny or dishonor his vicarious sacrifice: let us abide steadfast in this faith while others waver, and preach Christ crucified if all else forebear. Grace, mercy, and peace be to all who exalt Christ crucified!

Day 2

The Teaching of the Footwashing

> Jesus, knowing that the Father had given all things into his hands, and that he had come from God and was going back to God, rose from supper. He laid aside his outer garments, and taking a towel, tied it around his waist. Then he poured water into a basin and began to wash the disciples' feet and to wipe them with the towel that was wrapped around him.
>
> John 13:3–5

Our Lord washed the feet of his disciples to show that to the last moment of his time with them he was full of the deepest and truest love to them, and was willing to perform the most menial action for their good. Nor was this all, for we may regard that one condescending act as the pledge and type of his daily kindness towards all his own, which are in the world. Those deeds of love, which the foot washing sets forth, are continuous among us, and are the sure tokens of his abiding love to us. Our Lord's affection for his people is not a transient passion. He loved them before ever the earth was, he continues still to love them, and he always will love them when these heavens and this earth shall have passed away. In token of the continuance of his love, he has left on record this washing of his disciples' feet, not because he did it once only, but because it is the type of what he is always doing. Even in his glory he is caring for his saints with that same condescending love which led him to wash their feet, and he is acting towards them spiritually in the selfsame way.

The love of Christ will assuredly endure all the strain that can ever be put upon it, for at the time when he acted as menial servant to his disciples his love was enduring, and enduring right gloriously, three great trials, any one of which might have broken it had it not been altogether omnipotent. For, first, he was about to go away from them. Much of human love needs the presence of its object for its maintenance; it is, alas, seldom true that "absence makes the heart grow fonder." Jesus was about to depart out of this world unto the Father, and, with the exception of one brief interval, he was no more to walk in the midst of his chosen, or sit at table with them. Out of sight, however, they would not be out of mind. Though he was just about to take the last terrible journey of death, yet he forgot them not, but graciously made them see that he would remember them still.

If you will remember the style of his going, his thoughtfulness of his friends becomes the more remarkable. He was about to leave them by a cruel and ignominious death, and according to the common conduct of men it would not have been wonderful if he had sought pity and comfort from his friends; instead of which, he forgot himself and all the pain, and grief, and death which lay before him, and spent all his time and strength upon the comfort and establishment of his followers. When he knew that the hour was come when he must depart out of the world with pangs unutterable, he still loved his own with an all-absorbing love. There was much in the prospect of his grievous departure which might for a season have diverted his thoughts from them; but they lay so close to the center of his soul that even under such circumstances he washed their feet.

Next, it is to be remembered, that our Lord was well aware that one of his disciples had already entertained the idea of betraying him. There sat one at the table who had held a secret interview with the Pharisees and chief priests, and had taken money as a bribe for his Master's blood (Matthew 26:14–15). You cannot so dissociate a leading disciple from the rest as not to feel that the whole band was thereby disgraced, and the Lord might very well have said, "I will discard my apostles, for they have betrayed me;" especially when you recollect that those who did not sell him or betray him nevertheless all forsook him and fled, forsook him when they ought to have rallied round him, and have spoken up for him at the judgment seat. Like timid hares, they fled at the first bark of the dogs. It would not have been wonderful, had his been a human love, if he had said, "They are unworthy of me: their confidence dies out when they see my sorrow: they betray me, they forsake me, therefore I will let them go, and care for them no more."

No, but knowing what they were, our Lord took a towel and girded himself and washed their feet, yes, washed the traitor's feet, and gently handled that heel which had been lifted up against him; washing from it the dust gathered in its secret walk upon the traitor's errand. This act of tender, considerate affection, performed under such circumstances, to men who acted towards him in such ungenerous style, proves to us that his love will bear the strain of our ill-behavior, our want of fidelity, and our thousand grievous failures. Having loved his own, which are in the world, he loves them to the end.

There was a third strain, and a powerful one, too. Our Savior knew that the Father had committed all things into his hands, he knew that there was but a brief interval before he should die, and then he would ascend to the Father's right hand, and sit there eternally as God over all, blessed for evermore, yet he did not disdain to do a slave's work for his beloved ones.

Oftentimes circumstances alter affections. A man grows rich and great, and forgets his friends. This we would not suspect of Jesus if his had not been a greater change than we mortals can possibly experience; but his was a surpassing accession of glory: from being plunged in ignominy and shame he was exalted to receive the homage of angels, and the adoration of the whole universe. One would think that in the prospect of such honors, though he loved his own, he would not so love them as to become their servitor, and all in disarray stoop down before them, even to their feet, and do the service of a bondsman. No wonder that Peter raised an objection suggested by reverential awe. Who could without protest receive such humble service from such hands?

Yet our Lord did this with heaven's supernal glory descending on him! He disrobed himself, though angels longed to cast the imperial purple about his shoulders. With all things in his hand, he yet took a towel and wiped the disciples' feet.

Beloved, if our Lord's love bore these three strains, we may, like the apostle, be persuaded that neither death nor life, nor angels, nor principalities, nor powers, nor things present, nor things to come, nor height, nor depth, nor any other creature shall be able to separate us from the love of God which is in Christ Jesus our Lord (Romans 8:38–39).

Day 3
The Memorable Hymn

And when they had sung a hymn, they
went out to the Mount of Olives.
Matthew 26:30

It was customary, when the Passover was held, to sing, and this is the main reason why the Savior did so. During the Passover, it was usual to sing the 113th, and five following psalms, which were called the "Hallel." The first commences, you will observe, in our version, with "Praise ye the Lord!" or, "Hallelujah!" The 115th, and the three following, were usually sung as the closing song of the Passover.

Now, our Savior would not diminish the splendor of the great Jewish rite, although it was the last time that he would celebrate it. No; there shall be their holy beauty and delight of psalmody; none of it shall be stinted; the "Hallel" shall be full and complete. We may safely believe that the Savior sang through, or probably chanted, the whole of these six psalms; and my heart tells me that there was no one at the table who sang more devoutly or more cheerfully than did our blessed Lord. There are some parts of the 118th Psalm, especially, which strike us as having sounded singularly grand, as they flowed from his blessed lips. Note verses 22, 23, 24. Particularly observe those words, near the end of the Psalm, and think you hear the Lord himself singing them, "The LORD is God, and he has made his light to shine upon us. Bind the festal sacrifice with cords, up to the horns of the altar!

You are my God, and I will give thanks to you; you are my God; I will extol you. Oh give thanks to the LORD, for he is good; for his steadfast love endures forever!" (Psalm 118:27–29).

Because, then, it was the settled custom of Israel to recite or sing these psalms, our Lord Jesus Christ did the same; for he would leave nothing unfinished. Just as, when he went down into the waters of baptism, he said, "Thus it is fitting for us to fulfill all righteousness" (Matthew 3:15), so he seemed to say, when sitting at the table, "Thus it is fitting for us to fulfill all righteousness; therefore let us sing unto the Lord, as God's people in past ages have done." Beloved, let us view with holy wonder the strictness of the Savior's obedience to his Father's will, and let us endeavor to follow in his steps, in all things, seeking to be obedient to the Lord's Word in the little matters as well as in the great ones.

May we not venture to suggest another and deeper reason? Did not the singing of "a hymn" at the supper show the holy absorption of the Savior's soul in his Father's will? If, beloved, you knew that at—say, ten o'clock tonight, you would be led away to be mocked, and despised, and scourged, and that tomorrow's sun would see you falsely accused, hanging, a convicted criminal, to die upon a cross, do you think that you could sing tonight, after your last meal? I am sure you could not, unless with more than earth-born courage, and resignation your soul could say, "bind the festal sacrifice with cords, up to the horns of the altar" (Psalm 118:27). You would sing if your spirit were like the Savior's spirit; if, like him, you could exclaim, "Not as I will, but as you will" (Matthew 26:39); but if there should remain in you any selfishness, any desire to be spared the bitterness of death, you would not be able to chant the "Hallel" with the Master. Blessed Jesus, how wholly were you given up! how perfectly consecrated! so that, whereas other men sing when they are marching to their joys, you sang on the way to death, whereas other men lift up their cheerful voices when honor awaits them, you had, as brave, an holy sonnet on your lips when shame, and spitting, and death were to be your portion.

This singing of the Savior also teaches us the whole-heartedness of the Master in the work which he was about to do. The patriot warrior sings as he hastens to battle; to the strains of martial music he advances to meet the foeman; and even thus the heart, of our all-glorious Champion supplies him with song even in the dreadful hour of his solitary agony. He views the battle, but he dreads it not; though in the contest his sons will be "very sorrowful, even to death" (Matthew 26:38), yet before it, he is like Job's warhorse, "When the trumpet sounds, he says 'Aha!' He smells the battle from afar" (Job 39:25). He has a baptism to be baptized with, and he is straitened until it be accomplished (Luke 12:50). The Master does not go forth to the agony in the garden with a cowed and trembling spirit, all bowed and crushed in the dust; but he, advances to the conflict like a man who has his full strength about him—taken out to be, a victim (if I may use such a figure), not as a worn-out ox that has long borne the yoke, but as the firstling of the bullock, in the fullness of his strength. He goes forth to the slaughter, with his glorious undaunted spirit, fast and firm within him, glad to suffer for his people's sake, and for his Father's glory.

Let us, O fellow-heirs of salvation, learn to sing when our offering time comes, when our season for stern labor approaches; yes, let us pour forth a canticle of deep, mysterious, melody of bliss, when our dying hour is near at hand! Courage, brother! The waters are chilly; but fear will not by any means diminish the terrors of the river. Courage, brother! Death is solemn work; but playing the coward will not make it less so. Bring out the silver trumpet; let your lips remember the long-loved music, and let the notes be clear and shrill as you dip your feet in the Jordan: "Even though I walk through the valley of the shadow of death, I will fear no evil, for you are with me; your rod and your staff, they comfort me" (Psalm 23:4).

Day 4

The Agony in Gethsemane

And being in agony he prayed more earnestly; and his sweat became like great drops of blood falling down to the ground.
Luke 22:44

What was the cause of the peculiar grief of Gethsemane? Our Lord was the "man of sorrows and acquainted with grief" (Isaiah 53:3) throughout his whole life, and yet, though it may sound paradoxical, I scarcely think there existed on the face of the earth a happier man than Jesus of Nazareth, for the griefs which he endured were counterbalanced by the peace of purity, the calm of fellowship with God, and the joy of benevolence.

But in Gethsemane all seems changed, his peace is gone, his calm is turned to tempest. After supper our Lord had sung a hymn, but there was no singing in Gethsemane. Notice that all his life long you scarcely find him uttering an expression of grief, and yet here he says, not only by his sighs and by his bloody sweat, but in so many words, "My soul is very sorrowful, even to death" (Matthew 26:38). In the garden the sufferer could not conceal his grief, and does not appear to have wished to do so. Backward and forward thrice he ran to his disciples, he let them see his sorrow and appealed to them for sympathy; his exclamations were very piteous, and his sighs and groans were, I doubt not, very terrible to hear. Chiefly did that sorrow reveal itself in bloody sweat, which is a very unusual phenomenon, although I suppose we must believe those writers who record instances somewhat similar. The old physician Galen gives an instance in which, through extremity of horror, an individual poured forth a discolored sweat, so nearly crimson as at any rate to appear to have been blood. Other cases are given by medical authorities. We do not, however, on any previous occasion observe anything like this in our Lord's life; it was only in the last grim struggle among the olive trees that our Champion resisted unto blood, agonizing against sin. What ailed you, O Lord, that you should be so sorely troubled just then?

Do you suppose it was the fear of coming scorn, or the dread of crucifixion? Was it terror at the thought of death? Is not such a supposition impossible? Every man dreads death, and as man Jesus could not but shrink from it. When we were originally made we were created for immortality, and therefore to die is strange and uncongenial work to us, and the instincts of self-preservation cause us to start back from it; but surely in our Lord's case that natural cause could not have produced such specially painful results. It does not make even such poor cowards as we are sweat great drops of blood, why then should it work such terror in him? It is dishonoring to our Lord to imagine him less brave than his own disciples, yet we have seen some of the very feeblest of his saints triumphant in the prospect of departing. Read the stories of the martyrs, and you will frequently find them exultant in the near approach of the most cruel sufferings. The joy of the Lord has given such strength to them, that no coward thought has alarmed them for a single moment, but they have gone to the stake, or to the block, with psalms of victory upon their lips. Our Master must not be thought of as inferior to his boldest servants, it cannot be that he should tremble where they were brave. Oh, no; the noblest spirit among yon martyr-band is the Leader himself, who in suffering and heroism surpassed them all; none could so defy the pangs of death as the Lord Jesus, who, for the joy which was set before him, endured the cross, despising the shame.

What is it then, think you, that so peculiarly marks off Gethsemane and the griefs thereof? We believe that now the Father put him to grief for us. It was now that our Lord had to take a certain cup from the Father's hand. Not from the Jews, not from the traitor Judas, not from the sleeping disciples, not from the devil came the trial now, but it was a cup filled by one whom he knew to be his Father, but who nevertheless he understood to have appointed him a very bitter potion, a cup not to be drunk by his body and to spend its gall upon his flesh, but a cup which especially amazed his soul and troubled his inmost heart. He shrunk from it, and therefore be sure that it was a draught more dreadful than physical pain, since from that he did not shrink; it was a potion more dreadful than reproach, from that he had not turned aside; more dreadful than Satanic temptation—that he had overcome: it was a something inconceivably terrible, amazingly full of dread, which came from the Father's hand. This removes all doubt as to what it was, for we read "It was the will of the Lord to crush him; he has put him to grief; when his soul makes an offering for guilt" (Isaiah 53:10). "And the Lord has laid on him the iniquity of us all" (Isaiah 53:6). He hath made him to be sin for us though he knew no sin (2 Corinthians 5:21). This, then, is that which caused the Savior such extraordinary depression. He was now about to "taste death for everyone" (Hebrews 2:9) to bear the curse which was due to sinners, because he stood in the sinner's place and must suffer in the sinner's stead. Here is the secret of those agonies which it is not possible for me to set forth in order before you, so true is it that—

> 'Tis to God, and God alone,
> That his griefs are fully known.[4]

4. "Much We Talk of Jesus' Blood" by Joseph Hart, 1712–1768.

Day 5
The Betrayal

While he was still speaking, there came a crowd, and the man called Judas, one of the twelve, was leading them. He drew near to Jesus to kiss him, but Jesus said to him, "Judas, would you betray the Son of Man with a kiss?"
Luke 22:47–48

When Satan had been entirely worsted in his conflict with Christ in the garden, the man-devil Judas came upon the scene. As the Parthian[5] in his flight turns round to shoot the fatal arrow, so the archenemy aimed another shaft at the Redeemer, by employing the traitor into whom he had entered. Judas became the devil's deputy, and a most trusty and serviceable tool he was. The Evil One had taken entire possession of the apostate's heart, and, like the swine possessed of devils, he ran violently downwards towards destruction (John 13:2). Well had infernal malice selected the Savior's trusted friend to be his treacherous betrayer, for thus he stabbed at the very center of his broken and bleeding heart. But, beloved, as in all things God is wiser than Satan, and the Lord of goodness outwits the Prince of Evil, so, in this dastardly betrayal of Christ, prophecy was fulfilled, and Christ was the more surely declared to be the promised Messiah.

It is appointed that he must die, but how shall he fall into the hands of his adversaries? Shall they capture him

5. A reference to the military tactics of the ancient Parthians, who would routinely discharge arrows while in real or feigned retreat.

in conflict? It must not be, lest he appear an unwilling victim. Shall he flee before his foes until he can hide no longer? It is not meet that a sacrifice should be hunted to death. Shall he offer himself to the foe? That were to excuse his murderers, or be a party to their crime. Shall he be taken accidentally or unawares? That would withdraw from his cup the necessary bitterness which made it wormwood mingled with gall. No; he must be betrayed by his friend, that he may bear the utmost depths of suffering, and that in every separate circumstance there may be a well of grief.

One reason for the appointment of the betrayal lay in the fact that it was ordained that man's sin should reach its culminating point in his death. God, the great owner of the vineyard, had sent many servants, and the husbandmen had stoned one and cast out another; last of all, he said, "I will send my Son; surely they will reverence my Son." When they slew the heir to win the inheritance, their rebellion had reached its height (Matthew 21:33–40). The murder of our blessed Lord was the extreme of human guilt; it developed the deadly hatred against God which lurks in the heart of man. When man became a deicide, sin had reached its fullness; and in the black deed of the man by whom the Lord was betrayed, that fullness was all displayed.

If it had not been for a Judas, we had not known how black, how foul, human nature may become. I scorn the men who try to apologize for the treachery of this devil in human form, this son of perdition, this foul apostate. I should think myself a villain if I tried to screen him, and I shudder for the men who dare extenuate his crimes. My brethren, we should feel a deep detestation of this master of infamy; he has gone to his own place, and the anathema of David, part of which was quoted by Peter, has come upon him, "When he is tried, let him come forth guilty; let his prayer be counted as sin! May his days be few; may another take his office!" (Psalm 109:7–8). Surely, as the devil was allowed unusually to torment the bodies of men, even so was he let loose to get possession of Judas as he has seldom gained possession of any other man, that we might see how foul, how desperately evil is the human heart.

Beyond a doubt, however, the main reason for this was that Christ might offer a perfect atonement for sin. We may usually read the sin in the punishment. Man betrayed his God. Man had the custody of the royal garden, and should have kept its green avenues sacred for communion with his God; but he betrayed the trust; the sentinel was false; he admitted evil into his own heart, and so into the paradise of God. He was false to the good name of the Creator, tolerating the insinuation which he should have repelled with scorn. Therefore must Jesus find man a traitor to him. There must be the counterpart of the sin in the suffering which he endured. You and I have often betrayed Christ. We have, when tempted, chosen the evil and forsaken the good; we have taken the bribes of hell, and have not followed closely with Jesus. It seemed most fitting, then, that he who bore the chastisement of sin should be reminded of its ingratitude and treachery by the things which he suffered.

Besides, brethren, that cup must be bitter to the last degree which is to be the equivalent for the wrath of God. There must be nothing consolatory in it; pains must be taken to pour into it all that even Divine wisdom can invent of awful and unheard of woe, and this one point—"He who ate my bread has lifted his heel against me" (John 13:18), was absolutely necessary to intensify the bitterness. Moreover, we feel persuaded that by thus suffering at the hand of a traitor the Lord became a faithful High Priest, able to sympathize with us when we fall under the like affliction (Hebrews 4:15). Since slander and ingratitude are common calamities, we can come to Jesus with full assurance of faith; he knows these sore temptations, for he has felt them in their very worst degree. We may cast every care, and every sorrow upon him, for he cares for us, having suffered with us. Thus, then, in our Lord's betrayal, Scripture was fulfilled, sin was developed, atonement was completed, and the great all-suffering High Priest became able to sympathize with us in every point.

Day 6

Jesus Declining the Legions

"Do you think that I cannot appeal to my Father, and he will at once send me more than twelve legions of angels? But how then should the Scriptures be fulfilled, that it must be so?"
Matthew 26:53–54

He says, when about to be bound and taken away to Caiaphas, "I can presently call down twelve legions of angels from the skies." He had influence in heaven with the Father, the great Lord of angels. He could have of the Father all that the Father possessed. Heaven would be emptied if needful to satisfy the wish of the Beloved Son. The man Christ Jesus who is about to be hung upon the cross has such power with the Father that he has but to ask and to have. The Father would answer him at once: "He shall presently send me twelve legions of angels." There would be no delay, no hesitation. The Father was ready to help him, waiting to deliver him. All heaven was concerned about him. All the angelic bands were waiting on the wing, and Jesus had but to express the desire, and instantaneously the garden of Gethsemane would have been as populous with shining ones as the New Jerusalem itself.

Our Lord speaks of angels that his Father would give him, or send him. We may interpret it that the Father would at once put at his disposal the glorious inhabitants of heaven. Think of seraphs at the disposal of the Man of Sorrows! He is despised and rejected of men, and yet angels that excel in strength are at his beck and call. Swift of wing, and quick of hand, and wise of thought, they are charmed to be the messengers of the Son of Man, the servitors of Jesus. Think of this, beloved, when you bow before the thorn-crowned head, and when you gaze upon the nailed hands and feet. Remember that angels and principalities and powers, and all the ranks of pure spirits by whatsoever name they are named, were all at the beck of Jesus when he was newly risen from his agony, and was about to be led away bound, to the high priest. He is our Lord and God, even at his lowest and weakest.

Jesus speaks of "twelve legions." I suppose he mentions the number twelve as a legion for each one of the eleven disciples and for himself. They were only twelve, and yet the innumerable hosts of heaven would make forced marches for their rescue. A legion in the Roman army was six thousand men at the very lowest. Twelve times six thousand angels would come in answer to a wish from Jesus. Nay, he says, "more" than twelve legions. There can be no limit to the available resources of the Christ of God. Thousands of thousands would fill the air if Jesus willed it. The band that Judas led would be an insignificant squad to be swallowed up at once if the Savior would but summon his allies.

Behold, dear brethren, the glory of our betrayed and arrested Lord. If he was such then, what is he now, when all power is given him of his Father! Bear in your minds the clear idea that Jesus in his humiliation was nevertheless Lord of all things, and especially of the unseen world, and of the armies which people it. The more clearly you perceive this, the more will you admire the all-conquering, all-abjuring love which took him to the death of the cross.

Our Lord would be betrayed into the hands of sinners, but he would go with them willingly. He had not shunned the garden though Judas knew the place. No part of our Lord's sufferings came upon him by the necessity of his nature. Neither as God nor as sinless man was he bound to suffer. There was no necessity that Christ should endure any of the inflictions laid upon him, except the necessity of his fulfilling the Scriptures, and performing the work of mercy which he came to do. He must die because he became the great sacrifice for sin; but apart from that, no necessity of death was on him.

Wonderful is that question, "How then shall the scriptures be fulfilled?" It is as much as to say, "Who else can drink that cup? Who else can tread the winepress of Almighty wrath? No, I must do it. I cannot lay this load upon any other shoulders." Therefore, for the joy that was set before him he endured the cross, despising the shame (Hebrews 12:2). He was willing, ay, willing from beginning to end, to be our suffering Savior. He was willing to be born at Bethlehem, to work at Nazareth, to be mocked at Jerusalem, and at last to die at Calvary. At any one point he could have drawn back. No constraint was upon him but that of a love stronger than death.

I want you, dear hearers, to draw the inference that Jesus is willing to save. A willing Sufferer must be a willing Savior. If he willingly died, he must with equal willingness be ready to give to us the fruit of his death. If any of you would have Jesus, you may surely have him at once. He freely delivered himself up for us all. If he was so willing to become a sacrifice, how willing must he be that the glorious result of his sacrifice should be shared in by you, and by all who come to God by him!

If there be unwillingness anywhere, you are unwilling. He rejoices to be gracious. I wish the charm of this truth would affect your heart as it does mine. I love him greatly, because I see that at any moment he might have drawn back from redeeming me, and yet he would not. A single prayer would have set him free; but he would not pray it, for he loved us so!

Do not grieve him by thinking that he is unwilling to forgive, that he is unwilling to receive a sinner such as you. Has he not said, "whoever comes to me I will never cast out" (John 6:37)? You will delight him if you come to him, whoever you may be. If you will but draw near to him by simple trust, he will see in you the purchase of his agony; and all the merit of his death shall flow out freely to you. Come and welcome, sinner, come.

Day 7

The Greatest Trial on Record

The kings of the earth set themselves, and the rulers take counsel together, against the LORD and against his Anointed.
Psalm 2:2

This preliminary mockery being over, Caiaphas, the high priest came in; he began at once to interrogate the Lord before the public trial doubtless with the view of catching him in his speech. The high priest asked him first of his disciples. "Where are your gallant followers? If you are a good man, why are they not here to bear witness to you? Where are they gone? Are they not ashamed of their folly, now that your promises of honor all end in shame?" The high priest "questioned Jesus about his disciples" (John 18:19). Our Lord Jesus on this point said not a syllable. Why this silence? Because it is not for our Advocate to accuse his disciples. He might have answered, "Well do you ask, 'Where are they?' the cowards forsook me; when one proved a traitor, the rest took to their heels." But no, he would not utter a word of accusation; he whose lips are mighty to intercede for his people, will never speak against them. Let Satan slander, but Christ pleads. The accuser of the brethren is the prince of this world: the Prince of Peace is ever our Advocate before the eternal throne.

For the rest of the questioning, our Lord Jesus said not a word in self-defense; he knew that it availed not for a lamb to plead with wolves; he was well aware that whatever he said would be misconstrued and made a fresh source of accusation, and he willed, moreover, to fulfill the prophecy, "like a lamb that is led to the slaughter, and like a sheep that before its shearers is silent, so he opened not his mouth" (Isaiah 53:7). But what power he exerted in thus remaining silent! Perhaps nothing displays more fully the omnipotence of Christ, than this power of self-control. Control the Deity? What power less than divine can attempt the task? Behold, my brethren, the Son of God does more than rule the winds and commend the waves, he restrains himself. And when a word, a whisper, would have refuted his foes, and swept them to their eternal destruction, he "opened not his mouth." He who opened his mouth for his enemies, will not utter a word for himself. If ever silence were more than golden, it is this deep silence under infinite provocation.

But now the court are all sitting; the members of the great Sanhedrin are all in their various places, and Christ is brought forth for the public trial before the highest ecclesiastical court; though it is, mark you, a foregone conclusion, that by hook or by crook they will find him guilty. They scour the neighborhood for witnesses. There were fellows to be found in Jerusalem, like those who in the olden times frequented the Old Bailey,[6] "straw witnesses," who were ready to be bought on either side; and, provided they were well paid, would swear to anything.

But for all this, though the witnesses were ready to perjure themselves, they could not agree one with another; being heard separately, their tales did not tally. At last two came, with some degree of similarity in their

6. The Old Bailey is the nickname for the Central Criminal Court of England and Wales.

witness; they were both liars, but for once the two liars had struck the same note. They declared that he said, "I will destroy this temple that is made with hands, and in three days I will build another, not made with hands" (Mark 14:58). Even when thus misrepresented, the witness was not sufficient as the foundation of a capital charge. Surely there could be nothing worthy of death in a man's saying, "Destroy this temple, and I will build it in three days." A person might make use of those words a thousand times over—he might be very foolish, but he would not be guilty of death for such an offense. But where men have made up their minds to hate Christ, they will hate him without a cause.

Finding that their witness, even when tortured to the highest degree, was not strong enough, the high priest, to get matter of accusation, adjured him by the Most High God to answer whether he was the Christ, "the Son of the Blessed." Being thus adjured, our Master would not set us an example of cowardice; he spoke to purpose; he said, "I am," and then, to show how fully he knew this to be true, he added, "you will see the Son of Man seated at the right hand of Power, and coming with the clouds of heaven" (Mark 14:62). I cannot understand what Unitarians do with this incident. Christ was put to death on a charge of blasphemy, for having declared himself to be the Son of God. Was not that the time when any sensible person would have denied the accusation? If he had not really claimed to be the Son of God, would he not now have spoken? Would he not now, once for all, have delivered our minds from the mistake under which we are laboring, if, indeed, it be a mistake, that he is the Son of God? But no, he seals it with his blood; he bears open testimony before the herd of his accusers. "I am. I am the Son of God, and I am the sent-one of the Most High." Now, now the thing is done. They want no further evidence. The judge, forgetting the impartiality which becomes his station, pretends to be wonderfully struck with horror, rends his garments, turns round to ask his co-assessors whether they need any further witness, and they, all too ready, hold up their hands in token of unanimity, and he is at once condemned to die.

Ah! brethren, and no sooner condemned, than the high priest, stepping down from his divan, spits in his face, and then the Sanhedrin follow, and smite him on his cheek; and then they turn him down to the rabble that had gathered in the court, and they buffet him from one to the other, and spit upon his blessed cheeks, and smite him, and then they play the old game again, which they had learned so well before the trial came on; they blindfold him for a second time, place him in the chair, and as they smite him with their fists they cry, "Prophecy to us, you Christ! Who is it that struck you?" (Matthew 26:67–68). And thus the Savior passed a second time through that most brutal and ignominious treatment. If we had tears, if we had sympathies, if we had hearts, we should prepare to shed those tears, to awake those sympathies, and break those hearts, now. O thou Lord of life and glory! how shamefully were you mistreated by those who pretended to be the curators of holy truth, the conservators of integrity, and the teachers of the law!

Having thus sketched the trial as briefly as I could, let me just say, that, throughout the whole of this trial before the ecclesiastical tribunal, it is manifest that they did all they could to pour contempt upon his two claims—to deity and to messiahship. Now, friends, as truly as on that eventful occasion—you and I must range ourselves on one of two sides. Either this day we must cheerfully acknowledge his Godhead, and accept him also as the Messiah, the Savior promised of old to us; or else we must take our post with those who are the adversaries of God and of his Christ. Will you ask yourself the question, on which side will you now stand?

Day 8

A Winter's Evening

The servant girl at the door said to Peter, "You also are not one of this man's disciples, are you?" He said, "I am not." Now the servants and officers had made a charcoal fire, because it was cold, and they were standing and warming themselves. Peter also was with them, standing and warming himself.
John 18:17–18

One does not wonder at the high priest's servants making a fire of coals, for it was cold—and one is not surprised at their standing to warm their hands, for they knew but little, comparatively, of Christ. They had never tasted of his love, they had never seen his miracles, they had not been asked to watch with him in the garden of Gethsemane, they had never heard him say, "Blessed are you, Simon Bar-jonah! For flesh and blood has not revealed this to you" (Matthew 16:17); the marvel is that Peter should stand there among them warming his hands.

Why did he do so? Not because he was indifferent to his Master. Let us do him justice; it is plain that he was in a dreadful state of mind that night. He was so attached to his Master that he followed him up to the door of the hall, and stopped there till John came out, and admitted him. He went up to the fire because he thought he must act as others did, so as to escape suspicion, and as they warmed their hands, he did the same, so as to appear as one of them. It so happened, however, that the light of the fire shone upon his face, and lit up his countenance, so that one said, "You are one of his disciples." Then, to get away from observation, we find Peter passing into another part of the hall, where, I suppose, it was darker. The people were talking, and Peter must needs talk, for it was his weakness to do so, and, moreover, he might have been suspected again had he been silent. Then another remarked, "You also are of Galilee, for your speech betrays you." He was discovered again, and so made for the door, but was known there also. He was all in a tremble. He did love his Master, weak as his faith was, and therefore he could not leave him, and yet he was afraid to confess him. He was worried and troubled, tossed to and fro between a desire to rush forward and do some rash thing for his Lord and a fear of his own life. He went to the fire, because nobody would think that a follower of Jesus could warm his hands while his Master was being despitefully entreated.

You see the gist of my observation, that for a disciple of Christ to make his own ease and comfort the main thing is most palpably inconsistent with the Christian character. Ah, dear brethren, our Lord had not where to lay his head; though he was rich, yet for our sakes he became poor; can it be consistent for the Christian to make the getting of money the main business of life? Is such a disciple like his Master? The Master gives up everything, shall the disciple labor to aggrandize himself? May the Holy Spirit keep us from this!

Peter, if he had known it, was better off outside the door than in the hall. I suppose he had forgotten the Master's warnings; for if he had thought of them, he would have said to himself, "Peter, you had better go home. Did not Jesus, in fact, tell you to go home, when he said to those who came to seize him, 'If you seek me, let these men go'?" (John 18:8). It would seem to have been the path of humble obedience to have gone his way, and not to have pressed into the hall. Though no doubt the motives which led both Peter and John into the high priest's house were commendable, Peter's position among the soldiers and hangers-on around the fire was extremely full of peril, and offered no corresponding advantages. Did he not know that "evil communications corrupt good manners"? Did he not know that the men who had taken his Lord prisoner were not fit associates for him? Should he not have felt that, though he might have his hands warmed, he would be likely to get his heart blackened by mixing with such company?

Here was Peter warming his hands, and he thought that nobody would know him, but his face, as we said before, was illuminated by the light of the fire, and one said, "Surely you are one of his disciples." The fire did not merely warm, but it threw light on him, and showed him up; and so, when it comes to pass that a Christian gets into association with the ungodly, and figures with them, his sin will find him out. Peter tried to look uncommonly comfortable and calm while at the fire, but he could not do it; he discovered himself by the twitches of his face, and the very look of him; and when he spoke, as we have already said, the tones of his voice betrayed him. Ah, Christian man, you had better keep to your own company; it is of no use for you to try to travel incognito through this world, for it will detect you. Never go where you will be ashamed to be seen, for you will be seen. A city set on a hill cannot be hid; a lighted candle must be seen. In vain will you try to pass yourself off as a stranger to Christ, your speech will betray you, and the finger of scorn will be justly pointed at you for your inconsistency;

therefore, keep to your own company, and walk not in the way of the wicked.

A few coals in a brazier suffice to warm Peter's hands; but even the infinite love of Jesus did not just then warm his heart. O sirs, what was the scene at the end of the hill? Was not that enough to set all hearts aglow? It was a bush that burned with fire, and was not consumed. It was the Son of God smitten on the mouth, and vilely slandered, and yet bearing it all for love of us. O sirs, there was a furnace at the other end of the hall—a furnace of love divine! If Peter had but looked at his Master's face, marred with agony, and seen upon it the mark of his terrible night's sweat, surely, had his heart been right, it must have burned within him. One marvels that, with such a sight before him—if Peter had been Peter—if he had only been true to that true heart of his, he would have braved the malice of the throng, placed himself side by side with his Lord, and said, "Do to me whatever you do to him. If you smite him, smite me. Take me, and let me suffer with him." If he might not have done that, one would not have wondered if Peter had sat there and wept till he broke his heart to see his Master treated so. But, alas! the sight of his Lord, accused and betrayed, did not warm Peter's heart. My brethren, we sometimes wish that we had actually seen our Lord, but seeing Christ after the flesh was of small service to Peter. It was when the Holy Spirit used the glance of Jesus as a special means of grace that Peter's heart was thawed, and his eyes dropped with tears of repentance.

Day 9
Our Lord's First Appearance Before Pilate

Then Pilate said to him, "So you are a king?" Jesus answered, "You say that I am a king. For this purpose I was born and for this purpose I have come into the world—to bear witness to the truth. Everyone who is of the truth listens to my voice."
John 18:37

When the morning light had come, and they had gone through the formality of a set trial by daylight, having really condemned him in the night, they led Jesus away to Pilate. According to tradition, he was led with a rope about his neck, and his hands bound; and I can fully believe in the tradition when I remember the words of Isaiah: "He was led as a lamb to the slaughter" (Isaiah 53:7 NKJV). It was a strangely sad procession which moved through Jerusalem a little after six in the morning.

When they came to the house of the Roman governor, they would not themselves enter within its doors, because they must by no means be defiled by the touch of a Gentile, for they had already commenced to keep the Passover. So they waited in the courtyard, and Pilate condescended to come out to them and learn the pressing business which brought them there so early in the morning. The Roman governor was proud, and cruel, and abhorred the Jews; but still, knowing their fanaticism and the readiness with which they broke loose at Passover times, he stood at his palace gate and heard their demands, he soon ascertained that they had brought him a prisoner, evidently a poor man, and in personal appearance emaciated, weary, and suffering. About him there was a mysterious dignity combined with singular gentleness, and Pilate for this and other reasons evidently took a singular interest in him. Fixing his gaze first upon the extraordinary prisoner, he turned to the angry priests and demanded, "What accusation do you bring against this man?"

They said that he wrought sedition, that he forbade to pay tribute unto Caesar, and made himself out to be a king. These were three great lies, for Jesus had preached peace, and not sedition; his example was submission, not rebellion; his spirit was that of a servant, not that of a turbulent party leader. He had never said that men were not to pay tribute to Caesar; on the contrary, he had said, "Render to Caesar the things that are Caesar's" (Mark 12:17), and submitted himself to every ordinance of authority. He had never in their sense set himself up to be a king; if he had done so, many who were now his accusers might have been his partisans. The charge against Jesus of setting up to be a king in the sense in which they desired Pilate to understand them was utterly false, for when the multitude had been fed, they would have taken him and made him a king, but he hid himself (John 6:15). All his life long he had preached peace and love, and a kingdom which is righteousness and peace. He was no rival to Caesar, and they knew it.

But yet I want you to note very carefully that the Lord never denied this charge in the sense in which he chose to understand it. He first explained what he meant by his being a king, and when he had explained it then he openly confessed that it was even so. First, I say, he explained what he meant by being a king, and notice carefully that he did not explain it away. He said, "My kingdom," and also when Pilate said, "Are you a king then?" he said, "You say that I am a king." He was there and then a real king, and he avowed it without reserve.

We are constantly told that the kingdom of Christ is a spiritual kingdom, and this saying is true; but I would have you take heed that you do not spirit away his kingdom as if it were only a pious dream. Spiritual or not, the kingdom of Christ on earth is real and powerful. It is real nonetheless, but all the more, because it may fitly be called spiritual. Jesus is even now a king. He said, "I am a king." Some say that his kingdom is not yet, but is reserved for the latter days; but I affirm that he is a king today, and that even now Jehovah has set him as king upon the holy hill of Zion. I bless God that he has translated us "into the kingdom of his dear Son" (Colossians 1:13 KJV). Christ is the king of glory (Psalm 24:7–10). When I say, "Your kingdom come" (Matthew 6:10), I do not mean that it may begin to be set up on earth, but that it may continue to be set up in new places, may be extended and grow, for Jesus has at this very moment a kingdom upon the face of the earth, and they that know the truth belong to it, and recognize him as the royal witness by whom the kingdom of truth has been founded and maintained.

The world knows him not, but yet he has a kingdom in it which shall ere long break in pieces all other kingdoms. True and loyal hearts are to be found among the sons of men, and in them his name still wakes enthusiasm, so that for him they are prepared to live and die. Our Lord is every inch a king, he has his throne of grace, has his scepter of truth, his officers who, like himself, witness to the truth, and his armies of warriors who wrestle not with flesh and blood, and use no carnal weapons, but yet go forth conquering and to conquer. Our Lord has his palace wherein he dwells, his chariot in which he rides, his revenues, though they be not treasures of gold and silver, and his proclamations, which are law in his church. His reigning power affects the destiny of the world at this present moment far more than the counsels of the five great powers: by the preaching of the truth his servants shape the ages, and set up and cast down the thrones of earth. There is no prince so powerful as Jesus, and no empire so mighty as the kingdom of heaven. I know that I address many who desire in their hearts today that Christ and his truth may triumph, and they little mind what becomes of themselves. Let but his gospel spread and the principles of righteousness prevail; and as for us, let us live or die, it shall be a matter of small concern. O King, live forever, and we shall find our life in your life, and glory in promoting your glory, world without end. Such a spirit is of the truth, and we may assure ourselves that Jesus is our King.

Our Lord having explained his meaning, confessed that he was a King. This is that to which Paul refers when he says, "Christ Jesus, who in his testimony before Pontius Pilate made the good confession" (1 Timothy 6:13). He did not draw back and say, "I am no King." Pilate might have delivered him then; but he spoke boldly concerning his blessed, mysterious, and wonderful kingdom, and therefore it was not possible that he should be set free. This, indeed, was his accusation written over his cross, "This is Jesus, the King of the Jews" (Matthew 27:37).

Day 10
Our Lord Before Herod

When Herod saw Jesus, he was very glad, for he had long desired to see him, because he had heard about him, and he was hoping to see some sign done by him. So he questioned him at some length, but he made no answer.
Luke 23:8–9

It is said of Herod, in consequence of this curiosity, that he rejoiced to see Jesus. It is said that he was "exceeding glad." What a hopeful state to be in! May we not expect great things when a man sees Jesus and is exceeding glad? But it was a frivolous gladness, because he hoped that now his curiosity would be satisfied. He had Jesus in his power, and he hoped now to hear some of the oratory of the prophet of whom men said, "No one ever spoke like this man" (John 7:46). He hoped to see him work a miracle, even he, of whom the record was, "He has done all things well" (Mark 7:37). Could not the great prophet be induced to multiply loaves and fishes? Might he not persuade him to heal a blind beggar, or make a lame man leap as a hart? Would not a miracle make rare mirth in Herod's palace, and cause a new sensation in the mind of the worn-out debauchee?

When Jesus was set before him he began to ask him questions. "Then he questioned with him in many words, but he answered him nothing" (Luke 23:9 KJV). If Herod had wanted to believe, Jesus would have been ready enough to instruct; if Herod had possessed a broken heart, Jesus would have hastened with tender words to bind it up; if Herod had been a candid inquirer, if his doubts had been sincere and true, the faithful and true Witness, the Prince of the kings of the earth, would have been delighted to speak with him. But Jesus knew that Herod would not believe in him and would not take up his cross and follow him and therefore he would not waste words on a heartless, soulless profligate. All the Master did was to maintain an absolute silence in his presence; "and, let him question as he might, he answered him nothing."

Observe, that our Master had good reason for refusing to speak to Herod this time, over and above what I have mentioned; because he would not have it supposed that he yielded to the pomp and dignity of men. Jesus never refused an answer to the question of a beggar; but he would not gratify the curiosity of a king. Herod dreams that he has a right to ask whatever impertinent questions he may choose to invent but Jesus knows nothing of men's rights in such a matter: it is all grace with him, and to him the prince upon the throne is not an atom better than the peasant in the cottage, and so when Herod in all his pride and glory thinks full sure that Christ will pay deference to him and, perhaps, will pay him court to win his favor, Jesus disregards him. He wants nothing of the murderer of John the Baptist. Had Herod been the poorest and most loathsome leper throughout all Judea, had he been the meanest mendicant in the street, who was lame or blind, his voice would at once have been heard by the Lord of mercy; but he will not answer the prince who hopes for homage at his hands, nor feed the idle wishes of a crafty reprobate. What favor did he want at Herod's hand? He had not come to be set free; he had come to die, and therefore his face is set like a flint, and, with heroic courage, he answers him not a word.

Remember, it was no small sorrow to our Lord to be silent. You tell me that he appears majestic in his silence. It is even so; but the pain of it was acute. Can you speak well? Do you love to speak for the good of your fellow men, and do you know that when you speak full often your words are spirit and life to those who hear you? It will be very hard to feel compelled to refuse them a good word. Do not imagine that the Lord despised Herod as Herod despised the Lord. Ah, no! The pity of his soul went out to this poor frivolous creature who must needs make sport of the Savior's sufferings, and treat the Son of the Highest as though he were a court fool, who must play before him. The Savior's infinite love was breaking his heart; for he longed to bless his persecutor, and yet he must not speak, nor give forth a warning word. True, there was little need for words, for his very presence was a sermon which ought to have melted a heart of stone; but yet it cost the Savior a mighty effort to keep down the floodgates and hold in the blessed torrents of his holy speech, which would have flowed out in compassionate pleadings. Silent he must be; but the anguish of it I can scarcely tell. Sometimes to be permitted to speak a word is the greatest comfort you can have. Have you never been in such a state that if you could cry out, it would have been a relief to you? What anguish, then, to be forced to be as a dumb man! What woe to be forced to be silent with all these mockers about him, and yet to be pitying them all!

Do you not think that this peculiar silence of Jesus was a part of his anguish, in which he was bearing the punishment for your sins of the tongue? Ah me, ah me! Redeemed of the Lord, how often have you misused your speech by wanton words! How often have we uttered murmuring words, proud words, false words, words of despite [scorn] to holy things; and now our sins of the tongue are all coming upon him, and he must stand silent there and bear our penalty.

What was the result of this disappointment upon Herod? Idle curiosity curdles into derision. He thinks the man is a fool, if not an idiot, and he says so, and begins to deride him. With his men of war he mocks him, and "set him at nought" (Luke 23:11 KJV), which signifies to make nothing of him. He calls his soldiers and says, "Look at this creature: he will not answer a word to what I have to say: is he bereft of his senses? Rouse him up, and see." Then they mock and laugh and jest and jeer. "Here," says Herod, "he calls himself a king! Bring out one of my shining white robes, and put it on him: we will make a king of him." So they put it about his blessed person, and again heap contumely [contempt] upon him. Was it not strange—this decking him in a gorgeous robe of dazzling white? The medieval writers delight to dwell on the fact that Herod arrayed our Lord in white and afterwards Pilate clothed him in red. Is he not the lily of the valley and the rose of Sharon (Song of Solomon 2:1)? Is he not matchlessly white for innocence, and then gloriously red in his atoning blood? Thus, in their very mockery, they are unconsciously setting forth to us both his spotless holiness and his majestic royalty.

Day 11

Pilate and Ourselves Guilty of the Savior's Death

The governor again said to them, "Which of the two do you want me to release for you?" And they said, "Barabbas." Pilate said to them, "Then what shall I do with Jesus who is called Christ?" They all said, "Let him be crucified!"
Matthew 27:21–22

Pilate having a conscience which troubled him was exceedingly anxious not to put Jesus to death, and yet could not see how he could avoid doing so, seeing that the Jews threatened to accuse him of want of loyalty to Caesar, and that Caesar the gloomy tyrant Tiberius, who was unrelenting in his fury. After first sending his prisoner to Herod, he finds that he cannot escape in that way, and therefore he catches at a second hope. He tells the mob that the custom of the feast required that one prisoner should be released, and that the choice remained with them. He hopes that they will choose Jesus of Nazareth. A vain hope indeed!

It so happened that there was another Jesus in prison at the time, namely, Jesus Barabbas, who had been a murderer, and was guilty both of sedition and robbery. Pilate brings out the two, and he gives the Jews their choice. It would make a wonderful picture if it were really so, as a writer on the life of Christ suggests, that Pilate actually set the two individuals before the crowd. See there the dark-browed, scowling assassin, with fierce looks, and every mark of fury and hate upon his face, the man taken red-handed, familiar with blood, the brigand whose very profession was strife! There he stands like a wolf, and by his side is set the gentle Lamb of God. See there in his face and bearing all that is good, tender, benevolent, heroic. The incarnations of hate and love are before them; and Pilate gives the crowd their choice. Without hesitation they cry, "Not this man, but Barabbas." The murderer walks away free, and the innocent Jesus is left to die.

Have we not here, first of all, in this act of the deliverance of the sinner and the binding of the innocent, a sort of type of that great work which is accomplished by the death of our Savior? You and I may fairly take our stand by the side of Barabbas. We have robbed God of his glory; we have been seditious traitors against the government of heaven; if he who hates his brother be a murderer, we also have been guilty of that sin. Here we stand before the judgment seat; the Prince of Life is bound for us and we are suffered to go free. The Lord delivers us and acquits us, while the Savior, without spot or blemish, or shadow of a fault, is led forth to crucifixion. Two birds were taken in the rite of the cleansing of a leper. The one bird was killed, and its blood was poured into a basin; the other bird was dipped in this blood, and then, with its wings all crimson, it was set free to fly into the open field (Leviticus 14:4–7). The bird slain well pictures the Savior, and every soul that has by faith been dipped in his blood, flies upward towards heaven singing sweetly in joyous liberty, owing its life and its liberty entirely to him who was slain.

It comes to this, Barabbas must die or Christ must die; you the sinner must perish, or Christ Immanuel, the Immaculate, must die. He dies that we may be delivered. Oh! have we all a participation in such a deliverance today? And though we have been robbers, traitors, and murderers yet we can rejoice that Christ has delivered us from the curse of the law, having been made a curse for us?

There are doubtless many here who this day prefer Barabbas to our Lord Jesus Christ. I fear that some among you have not chosen Christ; but what have you chosen? Let me mention two or three objects of human choice, worthy to be ranked with Barabbas of old. Too many have chosen lust to be their delight: I will not paint the hideous monster; I have no colors. It is a foul and bestial thing: the cheek of modesty crimsons at the very mention of it. Yet, for the pleasures of wantonness, Christ is set aside.

Very frequently I meet with persons who have chosen another Barabbas instead of Jesus. Drink is the demon which enthralls millions. It is a vice which degrades men, and defaces the image of God in them. We insult the brutes when we say that a drunken man sinks to the level of the beasts; for the cattle never go so low as that. Alas, I have known men—ay, and women, too—who have been hearers of the gospel, and have in a measure felt its power, and yet for this sin they have sold their souls and given up their Savior. I say that they prefer the drink-demon to the holy Lord Jesus. Oh, shame, cruel shame that this should be selected in preference to him who loved us and gave himself for us!

"Well, well," says one, "I do not fall into that sin." No, my friend, but what is it that you do choose instead of Christ, for if you do not set him on the throne of your heart, you are choosing something else. Is it that you do not want to be a Christian because you wish to save yourself trouble and would be happy and comfortable and enjoy yourself? You do not choose any openly vicious way in particular, but you prefer to be moderately sinful and to take care of yourself, and save all care, thought, and anxiety about death and heaven and hell. You think that by leading a careless life you are happier than if you yielded yourself to Jesus. You are laboring under a mistake; but one thing is clear—self is your god, and that is a deity as groveling as any other. The idolater who worships a god of gold or silver, or even of stone or mud, is not quite so degraded as the man who worships himself. Self-worship is coming very low indeed. When I am my own god, or my belly is my god, can there be a lower depth? Think of it, and be ashamed.

Oh, I say again, in many a man's choice of what should be the object of his life, he sins precisely as they sinned who put away Jesus and chose Barabbas. I say no more. May the Holy Spirit send home this sadly convicting truth.

Day 12
The Crown of Thorns

And twisting together a crown of
thorns, they put it on his head.
Matthew 27:29

And now let us press into the guardroom, and look at our Savior wearing his crown of thorns. Here is the Christ, the generous, loving, tender Christ, treated with indignity and scorn; here is the Prince of Life and Glory made an object of derision by a ribald soldiery. Behold today the lily among thorns, purity lifting up itself in the midst of opposing sin. See here the sacrifice caught in the thicket, and held fast there, as a victim in our stead to fulfill the ancient type of the ram held by the bushes, which Abraham slew instead of Isaac.

They mocked his claims to be a king. "Aha," they seemed to say, "is this a king? It must be after some uncouth Jewish fashion, surely, that this poor peasant claims to wear a crown. Is this the Son of David? When will he drive Caesar and his armies into the sea, and set up a new state, and reign at Rome? This Jew, this peasant, is he to fulfill his nation's dream, and rule over all mankind?" Wonderfully did they ridicule this idea, and we do not wonder that they did, for they could not perceive his true glory. Nor was it merely mockery, but cruelty added pain to insult. If they had only intended to mock him they might have platted [braided] a crown of straw, but they meant to pain him, and therefore they fashioned a crown of thorns.

Look, I pray you, at his person as he suffers under their hands. They had scourged him till probably there was no part of his body which was not bleeding beneath their blows except his head, and now that head must be made to suffer too. Alas, our whole head was sick, and our whole heart faint, and so he must be made in his chastisement like to us in our transgression. There was no part of our humanity without sin, and there must be no part of his humanity without suffering. If we had escaped in some measure from iniquity, so might he have escaped from pain, but as we had worn the foul garment of transgression, and it covered us from head to foot, even so must he wear the garments of shame and derision from the crown of his head even to the sole of his foot.

But the coronation of Christ with thorns was symbolical, and had great meaning in it, for, first, it was to him a triumphal crown. Christ had fought with sin from the day when he first stood foot to foot with it in the wilderness up to the time when he entered Pilate's hall, and he had conquered it. As a witness that he had gained the victory, behold sin's crown seized as a trophy! What was the crown of sin? Thorns. These sprang from the curse. "Thorns and thistles it shall bring forth for you" (Genesis 3:18) was the coronation of sin, and now Christ has taken away its crown, and put it on his own head. He has spoiled sin of its richest regalia, and he wears it himself. Glorious Champion, all hail!

What if I say that the thorns constituted a mural crown?[7] Paradise was set round with a hedge of thorns so sharp that none could enter it, but our Champion leaped first upon the bristling rampart, and bore the bloodred banner of his cross

7. A crown or garland given to the soldier who was first to scale the wall of a besieged town.

into the heart of that better new Eden, which thus he won for us never to be lost again. Jesus wears the mural chaplet which denotes that he has opened Paradise.

It was a wrestler's crown he wore, for he wrestled not with flesh and blood, but with principalities and powers, and he overthrew his foe.

It was a racer's crown he wore, for he had run with the mighty and outstripped them in the race. He had well-nigh finished his course, and had but a step or two more to take to reach the goal.

It was a crown rich with glory, despite the shame which was intended by it. We see in Jesus the monarch of the realms of misery, the chief among ten thousand sufferers. Jesus is the prince of martyrs. He leads the vanguard among the noble army of suffering witnesses and confessors of the truth. Though they died at the stake, or pined in dungeons, or were cast to wild beasts, none of them claim the first rank; but he, the faithful and the true witness, with the thorn crown and the cross, stands at the head of them all.

It may never be our lot to join the august band, but if there be an honor for which we might legitimately envy saints of former times, it is this, that they were born in those brave days when the ruby crown was within human grasp, and when the supreme sacrifice might have been made. We are cravens, indeed, if in these softer days we are ashamed to confess our Master, and are afraid of a little scorn, or tremble at the criticisms of the would-be wise. Rather let us follow the Lamb wherever he goes, content to wear his crown of thorns that we may in his kingdom behold his glory.

Day 13
Mocking the King

And kneeling before him, they mocked him, saying, "Hail, King of the Jews!" And they spit on him and took the reed and struck him on the head.
Matthew 27:29–30

Brethren and sisters in Christ, we have before us a King, and such a King as was never known before; his pedigree more glorious than that of any mere earthly monarch; his right to reign indisputable; his power to subdue all to himself infinite, whether he chose to use it or not, his character such as never belonged to any king before, as eminent in goodness as he was supreme in power, "the Son of the Most High" (Luke 1:32), "who is God over all, blessed forever" (Romans 9:5), yet who became the Son of Man for our sakes. This is the King who is now before us.

But what an enthronement was accorded to him! See that scarlet robe; it is a contemptuous imitation of the imperial purple that a king wears. See that old chair into which the soldiers have thrust him, so that he may be seated upon a mockery of a throne. See, above all, that crown upon his head. It has rubies in it, but the rubies are composed of his own blood, forced from his blessed temples by the cruel thorns. See, they pay him homage; but the homage is their own filthy spittle which runs down his cheeks. They bow the knee before him, but it is only in mockery. They salute him with the cry, "Hail, King of the Jews!" but it is done in scorn. Was there ever grief like his? It amazes us that such superlative goodness should have been treated with such fiendish malice, that such mercy should have been in such misery, that such majesty should have been reduced to such despising.

Truly, he was "despised and rejected by men, a man of sorrows and acquainted with grief" (Isaiah 53:3); and they do not exaggerate who speak of him as the emperor of sorrow and the enthroned prince of misery. Look at him, and then restrain your tears if you can. Gaze upon him, you who love him, and who know how fair was his glorious countenance before it was marred more than the face of any man, and see it all bestained with his own blood, and then let your heart delight if it can; nay, rather let me say, indulge your griefs, and let your sorrow flow in copious streams, for of all spectacles that were ever witnessed by human eyes, this surely is the most grievous.

But remember that, Jesus Christ stood in the sinner's place. This is an old truth, with which you are very familiar, but of which you are never tired of hearing. Having been "born in the likeness of men. And being found in human form" (Philippians 2:7–8), and having agreed to stand in the room and place of sinners as if he had been himself a sinner, you see in Jesus Christ the full result of sin epitomized. Man wanted to be a king, or to be more than a king. "You will be like God" (Genesis 3:5), said the serpent to Eve in the garden of Eden, insinuating that the great God was jealous of man, and fearful that man would grow so great as to be his rival. Thus tempted, man put out his hand, and touched the fruit whereof he had been forbidden to partake. He had been a happy subject, but he hoped that he might become a happier king. It had been his delight to do the will of the Lord, but now he thought he should be able to do his own will, and that he should be able to reign side by side with God, or even in his place.

Ah, foolish man, see what kind of royalty it is that sin can bring you! Come here, and see as in a glass the image of the coronation which sin gives to man. See how it crowns him with mock dignity and honor. It makes him look like a king, but it is only a tinsel splendor, all outside show and sham. It gives him no royal rank or regal character in any case whatever. It is true that there is a crown upon man's head, but it is a crown of thorns, and this is the only crown that sin can ever give to poor humanity. Man wanted to be lord of the earth, and so he was in a certain sense; but his first act of lordship was to cause a blast and blight upon paradise, and to sow the earth with thorns and thistles, so that thenceforth he should never even eat bread without being reminded of his sin through the very sweat on his face. O yes, man, you are a king! I can see your crown; set great store by it if you can proud, foolish monarch! You scorned to be a subject of the great Ruler of the universe, and now you have become yourself a monarch! Behold your royal regalia! Specially notice your crown—a crown of thorns! This is how sin crowns us. We see the same thing in our Savior, when he stood in our place, he was mocked, despised, rejected, and crowned with thorns, and this is what we become through sin. "Sin when it is fully grown brings forth death" (James 1:15). Christ on the cross is a yet fuller type of what man would have become had sin been let alone. It brings manhood ever lower and lower until it plucks his very life out of him, and lays him dead beneath the clods of the valley. Sin's only throne is a mock one, its only crown is a painful one, and its only reward is sorrow and shame. In Jesus, mocked by the soldiers, we see what sin had brought our race to and all that sin could do for us.

Day 14
The Great Cross-Bearer

So they took Jesus, and he went out, bearing his own cross, to the place called The Place of a Skull, which in Aramaic is called Golgotha.
John 19:16–17

We are told by John that our Savior "went forth bearing his cross." We might have supposed, so far as the other three evangelists are concerned, that Simon the Cyrenian had carried the cross all the way (Mark 15:21), but John fills up the blank space in their accounts. Our Lord carried his own cross at the commencement of the sorrowful pilgrimage to Calvary. Usually only one beam of the cross was carried: it may have been so now. It does not look so, however; for the expression, "bearing his cross," would naturally mean the whole of it.

If Simon had carried Christ's cross all the way, we should have missed the type of Isaac, for Isaac when he went to Mount Moriah to be offered up by his father carried the wood for his own sacrifice (Genesis 22:6). I think if I had been a Jew, full of hate to Jesus Christ, I would have said, "Do not let him carry his cross: that will be too much like Isaac carrying the wood." No; but knowing the type, they wantonly fulfill it. It is their own will that does it, and yet the predestination of the Eternal is fulfilled in every jot and tittle, and our great Isaac carries the wood with which he is to be offered up by his Father. How marvelous it is that there should be a fixed decree and yet an altogether unlimited free agency.

The spiritual meaning of it, of course, was that Christ in perfect obedience was then carrying the load of our disobedience. The cross, which was the curse, for "Cursed is everyone who is hanged on a tree" (Galatians 3:13), is borne on those blessed shoulders which were submissive to the will of God in all things. Our Lord's cross-bearing is the representation of his bearing all our sin, and therefore in it we rejoice.

The direction in which he is led is outside the city. He must not die in Jerusalem, though multitudes of prophets had perished there (Matthew 23:37). Though the temple was the central place of sacrifice, yet must not the Son of God be offered there, for he was an offering of another kind, and must not lie upon their altars. Outside the city, because by the Jews he was treated as a flagrant offender who must be executed at the Tyburn of the city,[8] in the appointed place of doom known as Calvary or Golgotha. When Naboth was unjustly condemned for blasphemy, they carried him forth out of the city, and stoned him with stones that he died (1 Kings 21:13); and afterwards Stephen—when they cried out against him as a blasphemer, they cast him out of the city, and there they stoned him (Acts 7:58). Our Savior therefore must die in the ordinary place of execution, that in all respects he might be numbered with the transgressors (Isaiah 53:12).

He was led outside of the city because from that time no acceptable sacrifice could be offered there. They might go on with their offering of daily lambs, and they

8. Tyburn was a site for public executions in London for over six hundred years, with the last one taking place in 1783.

might sacrifice their bullocks, and burn the fat of fed beasts; but from that day the substance of the sacrifice had gone away from them, and Israel's offerings were vain oblations. Because the true sacrifice is rejected of them the Lord leaves them nothing but a vain show. Still more forcible is the fact that our Lord must die outside the city because he was to be consumed as a sin-offering. There were several sorts of offerings under the law: the sweet-savor offerings were presented upon the altar, and were accepted of God, but sin-offerings were burnt without the camp or gate, because God can have no fellowship with sin (Exodus 29:14). Once let sin be imputed to the sacrifice and it becomes abhorrent to God, and must not be presented in the tabernacle or the temple, but burned outside the circle wherein his people have their habitations. And here let our hearts gratefully contemplate how truly our Lord Jesus became a sin-offering for us, and how in every point he followed out the type. With his face turned away from his Father's house he must go to die: with his face turned away from what were once his Father's people he must be led forth to be crucified.

Like a thing accursed, he is to be hung up where felons suffer condign [deserved] punishment. Because we were sinners, and because sin had turned our backs to God, and because sin had broken our communion with God's accepted ones, therefore must he endure this banishment. In that sorrowful march of the cross-bearing Savior, my soul with sorrow sees herself represented as deserving thus to be made to depart unto death; and yet joy mingles with this emotion, for the glorious Sin-bearer has thus taken away our sin, and we return from our exile: his substitution is infinitely effectual. Well may those live for whom Jesus died. Well may those retain in whose place the Son of God was banished. There is entrance into the holy city now, there is entrance into the temple now, there is access unto God himself now, because the Lord has put away our sin through him who was led to be crucified outside the city gate.

Nor do I think that even this exhausts the teaching. Jesus dies outside Jerusalem because he died, not for Jerusalem alone, nor for Israel alone. The effect of his atonement is not circumscribed by the walls of a city nor by the bounds of a race. In him shall all the nations of the earth be blessed. Out in the open he must die, to show that he reconciled both Jews and Gentiles unto God. "He is the propitiation for our sins," saith Paul, who was himself a Jew, "and not for ours only but also for the sins of the whole world" (1 John 2:2). Had he been the Savior of Jews only, seclusion in the place of his offering would have been appropriate, but as he dies for all nations, he is hung up without the city.

Day 15

The Determination of Christ to Suffer for His People

And they offered him wine mixed with
myrrh, but he did not take it.
Mark 15:23

Our Savior, before he was nailed to the cross, and on the cross, several times had drinks of different sorts offered to him. Whilst they were nailing him to the cross, they endeavored to make him drink wine, or vinegar as it is called, mingled with gall; and when he had tasted of it—he did taste it—he would not drink it (Matthew 27:34). When he was on the cross, the soldiers, mocking him, offered him vinegar, or their weak drink of which they ordinarily partook, pledging him in their cups with scorn (Luke 23:36). And once more, when he said, "I thirst," they took a sponge filled with vinegar, dipped it in hyssop, and put it to his lips (John 19:28–30).

This occasion of offering the wine mingled with myrrh is, I believe, different from all the rest. This wine mingled with myrrh was given to him as an act of mercy. Matthew Henry seems to think that it was prepared by those holy women who were wont to attend to the necessities of our Lord. It was these holy women who prepared the spices to embalm him at his burial. Prompted by their compassion for him, they got ready this cup of wine mingled with myrrh, that he might be strengthened for his miseries, and that those miseries might in some degree be alleviated by the partial stupefaction which a strong draught of wine and myrrh would give to him. This time, our Savior positively declined the cup: "he received it not." The wormwood he tasted, but this he received not at all; he would have nothing to do with it. Why? There is a glorious idea couched in the fact that the Savior put the myrrhed wine cup entirely away from his lips.

On the heights of heaven the Son of God stood of old, and he looked down and measured how far it was to the utmost depths of misery; he cast up the sum total of all the agonies which a man must endure to descend to the utmost depths of pain and misery. He determined that, to be a faithful High Priest, and also to be a suffering one, he would go the whole way, from the highest to the lowest, "from the highest throne in glory to the cross of deepest woe."[9] This myrrhed cup would just have stopped him within a little of the utmost limit of misery; therefore, he said, "I will not stop halfway, but I will go all the way; and if this cup can mitigate my sorrow, that is just the reason why I will not drink it, for I have determined that to the utmost lengths of misery I will go, that I will do, and bear, and suffer all that incarnate God can bear for my people, in my own mortal body." You will observe this fact that, in all the history of Christ, never once did he take anything which could have lessened his miseries, but he went the whole length; and as on this occasion he refused the wine drugged with myrrh, so never did he receive anything that had a tendency to prevent him from going to the requisite lengths of suffering.

---

9. "Mighty God, While Angels Bless Thee," by Robert Robinson, 1735–1790.

I do think that, if our Savior had drunk this myrrhed cup, the atonement would not have been valid. It strikes me that, if he had drunk this wine mingled with myrrh, he could not have suffered to the extent that was absolutely necessary. We believe Christ did, on the cross, suffer just enough, and not one particle more than was necessary for the redemption of his people. If, then, this wine cup had taken away a part of his sufferings, the ransom price would not have been fully complete, it would not have been fully paid. And if it had but taken away so much as a grain, the atonement would not have been sufficiently satisfactory. If a man's ransom is to be paid, it must be all paid; for though but one single farthing be left unpaid, the man is not fully redeemed, and he is not yet totally free. If, then, this drinking of the wine cup had taken out the smallest amount from that fearful price of agony which our Savior paid, the atonement would have been insufficient—insufficient only to a degree, but even insufficiency to a degree, however small, would have been enough to have caused perpetual despair, yea, enough to have shut the gates of heaven against all believers. The utmost farthing must be paid; inexorable justice never did yet omit so much as a fraction of its claim. Nor would it in this case have exonerated in any measure; Christ must pay it all. The wine cup would have prevented his doing that. Therefore, he would suffer and go the whole length of suffering; he would not stop, but would go through it all.

This suffering to the utmost was necessary to perfect his character as "a merciful High Priest" who has to compassionate souls that have gone to the utmost of miseries themselves; that he might know how to succor them that are tempted (Hebrews 4:15–16). O blessed Lord Jesus, you were "tempted in all points like as we are"! Blessed be your name! This myrrh-cup could have put a plate of steel upon your breast, it would have blunted many darts of suffering; therefore you put it aside that you might, naked, suffer every shaft to find its target in your heart. This myrrh-cup would have steeled your feelings, so that you could not be rent by the whips of anguish; therefore you would not take its steeling influence, its hardening qualities. You, who stooped to become a poor, weak worm, "a worm and not a man" (Psalm 22:6), did bear the agony, without making the agony less, or strengthening your own body to bear it. O blessed High Priest! Go to him, you tried and tempted ones; go to him, and cast your burdens on him; he can bear them, he has borne burdens heavier than yours before. Cast your burden on the Lord, as his shoulders can sustain it; and his shoulders, that have borne trouble without comfort, can bear your troubles, though they be comfortless ones, too. Do but tell them to your Master, and you shall never find a lack of sympathy in him.

Day 16
The First Cry from the Cross

And Jesus said, "Father, forgive them, for they know not what they do."
Luke 23:34

Our Lord was at that moment enduring the first pains of crucifixion; the executioners had just then driven the nails through his hands and feet. He must have been, moreover, greatly depressed, and brought into a condition of extreme weakness by the agony of the night in Gethsemane, and by the scourgings and cruel mockings which he had endured all through the morning, from Caiaphas, Pilate, Herod, and the Praetorian guards. Yet neither the weakness of the past, nor the pain of the present, could prevent him from continuing in prayer. The Lamb of God was silent to men, but he was not silent to God. Dumb as a sheep before her shearers, he had not a word to say in his own defense to man, but he continues in his heart crying unto his Father, and no pain and no weakness can silence his holy supplications. Beloved, what an example our Lord herein presents to us!

More remarkable, however, is the fact that our Lord's prayer to his Father was not for himself. He continued on the cross to pray for himself, it is true, and his lamentable cry, "My God, my God, why have you forsaken me" (Psalm 22:1), shows the personality of his prayer; but the first of the seven great cries on the cross has scarcely even an indirect reference to himself. It is, "Father, forgive them." The petition is altogether for others, and though there is an allusion to the cruelties which they were exercising upon himself, yet it is remote; and you will observe, he does not say, "I forgive them"—that is taken for granted—he seems to lose sight of the fact that they were doing any wrong to himself, it is the wrong which they were doing to the Father that is on his mind, the insult which they are paying to the Father, in the person of the Son; he thinks not of himself at all. The cry, "Father, forgive them," is altogether unselfish. He himself is, in the prayer, as though he were not; so complete is his self-annihilation, that he loses sight of himself and his woes. My brethren, if there had ever been a time in the life of the Son of Man when he might have rigidly confined his prayer to himself, without any one caviling thereat, surely it was when he was beginning his death throes. We could not marvel, if any man here were fastened to the stake, or fixed to a cross, if his first, and even his last and all his prayers, were for support under so arduous a trial. But see, the Lord Jesus began his prayer by pleading for others. Do you not see what a great heart is here revealed! What a soul of compassion was in the Crucified! How Godlike, how divine! Was there ever such a one before him, who, even in the very pangs of death, offers as his first prayer an intercession for others?

There is, however, a crowning jewel in this diadem of glorious love. The Sun of Righteousness sets upon Calvary in a wondrous splendor; but amongst the bright colors which glorify his departure, there is this one—the prayer was not alone for others, but it was for his cruelest enemies. His enemies, did I say, there is more than that to be considered. It was not a prayer for enemies who had done him an ill deed years before, but for those who were there and then murdering him. Not in cold blood did the Savior pray, after he had forgotten the injury, and could the more easily forgive it, but while the first red drops of blood were spurting on the hands which drove the nails; while yet the hammer was bestained with crimson gore, his blessed mouth poured out the fresh warm prayer, "Father, forgive them, for they know not what they do." I say, not that that prayer was confined to his immediate executioners. I believe that it was a far-reaching prayer, which included Scribes and Pharisees, Pilate and Herod, Jews and Gentiles—yes, the whole human race in a certain sense, since we were all concerned in that murder; but certainly the immediate persons, upon whom that prayer was poured like precious nard, were those who there and then were committing the brutal act of fastening him to the accursed tree. How sublime is this prayer if viewed in such a light! It stands alone upon a mount of solitary glory.

No other had been prayed like it before. It is true, Abraham, and Moses, and the prophets had prayed for the wicked; but not for wicked men who had pierced their hands and feet. It is true, that Christians have since that day offered the same prayer, even as Stephen cried, "Lord, do not hold this sin against them" (Acts 7:60); and many a martyr has made his last words at the stake words of pitying intercession for his persecutors; but you know where they learnt this, let me ask you where did he learn it? Was not Jesus the divine original? He learnt it nowhere; it leaped up from his own Godlike nature. A compassion peculiar to himself dictated this originality of prayer; the inward royalty of his love suggested to him so memorable an intercession, which may serve us for a pattern, but of which no pattern had existed before.

He prayed for his enemies then, he is praying for his enemies now; the past on the cross was an earnest of the present on the throne. He is in a higher place, and in a nobler condition, but his occupation is the same; he continues still before the eternal throne to present pleas on the behalf of guilty men, crying, "Father, O forgive them." All his intercession is in a measure like the intercession on Calvary, and Calvary's cries may help us to guess the character of the whole of his intercession above.

Day 17
The Dying Thief in a New Light

But the other rebuked him, saying, "Do you not fear God, since you are under the same sentence of condemnation? And we indeed justly, for we are receiving the due reward of our deeds; but this man has done nothing wrong." And he said, "Jesus, remember me when you come into your kingdom."
Luke 23:40–42

I greatly question whether the equal and the parallel of the dying thief's faith will be readily found outside the Scriptures, or even in the Scriptures. Observe, that this man believed in Christ when he literally saw him dying the death of a felon, under circumstances of the greatest personal shame.

You have never realized what it was to be crucified. None of you could do that, for the sight has never been seen in our day in England. There is not a man or woman here who has ever realized in their own mind the actual death of Christ. It stands beyond us. This man saw it with his own eyes, and for him to call him "Lord" who was hanging on a gibbet, was no small triumph of faith. For him to ask Jesus to remember him when he came into his kingdom, though he saw that Jesus bleeding his life away, and hounded to the death, was a splendid act of reliance. For him to commit his everlasting destiny into the hands of One who was, to all appearance, unable even to preserve his own life, was a noble achievement of faith. I say that this dying thief leads the vanguard in the matter of faith, for what he saw of the circumstances of the Savior was calculated to contradict rather than help his confidence. What he saw was to his hindrance rather than to his help, for he saw our Lord in the very extremity of agony and death, and yet he believed in him as the King shortly to come into his kingdom.

Recollect, too, that at that moment when the thief believed in Christ, all the disciples had forsaken him and fled. John might be lingering at a little distance, and holy women may have stood farther off, but no one was present bravely to champion the dying Christ. Judas had sold him, Peter had denied him, and the rest had forsaken him; and it was then that the dying thief called him "Lord," and said, "Remember me when you come into your kingdom." I call that splendid faith. Why, some of you do not believe, though you are surrounded with Christian friends—though you are urged on by the testimony of those whom you regard with love; but this man, all alone, comes out, and calls Jesus his Lord! No one else was confessing Christ at that moment; no revival was around him with enthusiastic crowds; he was all by himself as a confessor of his Lord. After our Lord was nailed to the tree, the first to bear witness for him was this thief. The centurion bore witness afterwards, when our Lord expired; but this thief was a lone confessor, holding on to Christ when nobody would say "Amen" to what he said. Even his fellow-thief was mocking at the crucified Savior, so that this man shone as a lone star in the midnight darkness. O sirs, dare you be Daniels? Dare you stand alone? Would you dare to stand out amidst a ribald crew, and say, "Jesus is my King. I only ask him to remember me when he comes into his kingdom"? Would you be likely to avow such a faith when priests and scribes, princes and people, were all mocking at the

Christ, and deriding him? Brethren, the dying robber exhibited marvelous faith, and I beg you to think of this next time you speak of him.

And it seems to me that another point adds splendor to that faith, namely, that he himself was in extreme torture. Remember, he was crucified. It was a crucified man trusting in a crucified Christ. Oh, when our frame is racked with torture, when the tenderest nerves are pained, when our body is hung up to die by we know not what great length of torment, then to forget the present and live in the future is a grand achievement of faith! While dying, to turn one's eye to Another dying at your side, and trust your soul with him, is very marvelous faith. Blessed thief, because they put you down at the bottom, as one of the least of saints, I think that I must bid you come up higher and take one of the uppermost seats among those who by faith have glorified the Christ of God!

Why, see, dear friends, once more, the speciality of this man's faith was that he saw so much, though his eyes had been opened for so short a time! He saw the future world. He was not a believer in annihilation, or in the possibility of a man's not being immortal. He evidently expected to be in another world, and to be in existence when the dying Lord should come into his kingdom. He believed all that, and it is more than some do nowadays. He also believed that Jesus would have a kingdom, a kingdom after he was dead, a kingdom though he was crucified. He believed that he was winning for himself a kingdom by those nailed hands and pierced feet. This was intelligent faith, was it not? He believed that Jesus would have a kingdom in which others would share, and therefore he aspired to have his portion in it. But yet he had fit views of himself, and therefore he did not say, "Lord, let me sit at your right hand;" or, "Let me share of the dainties of your palace;" but he said only, "Remember me. Think of me. Cast an eye my way. Think of your poor dying comrade on the cross at your right hand. Lord, remember me. Remember me." I see deep humility in the prayer and yet a sweet, joyous, confident exaltation of the Christ at the time when the Christ was in his deepest humiliation.

Oh, dear sirs, if any of you have thought of this dying thief only as one who put off repentance, I want you now to think of him as one that did greatly and grandly believe in Christ; and oh, that you would do the same! Oh, that you would put a great confidence in my great Lord! Never did a poor sinner trust Christ too much. There was never a case of a guilty one, who believed that Jesus could forgive him, and afterwards found that he could not—who believed that Jesus could save him on the spot, and then woke up to find that it was a delusion. No; plunge into this river of confidence in Christ. The waters are waters to swim in, not to drown in. Never did a soul perish that glorified Christ by a living, loving faith in him. Come, then, with all your sin, whatever it may be, with all your deep depression of spirit, with all your agony of conscience. Come along with you, and grasp my Lord and Master with both the hands of your faith, and he shall be yours, and you shall be his.

Day 18

Let Him Deliver Him Now

"He trusts in God; let God deliver him now, if he desires him. For he said, 'I am the Son of God.'"
Matthew 27:43

Such a test will come to all believers. It may come as a taunt from enemies; it will certainly come as a trial of your faith. The archenemy will assuredly hiss out, "Let him deliver him, seeing he delighted in him" (Psalm 22:8 KJV).

It is peculiarly painful to have this stern inference driven home to you in the hour of sorrow. Because one cannot deny the fairness of the appeal, it is all the more trying. In the time of depression of spirit it is hard to have one's faith questioned, or the ground on which it stands made a matter of dispute. Either to be mistaken in one's belief, or to have no real faith, or to find the ground of one's faith fail is an exceedingly grievous thing. Yet as our Lord was not spared this painful ordeal, we must not expect to be kept clear of it, and Satan knows well how to work these questions, till the poison of them sets the blood on fire. "He trusted on the LORD that he would deliver him; let him deliver him;" he hurls this fiery dart into the soul, till the man is sorely wounded, and can scarcely hold his ground.

The taunt is specially pointed and personal. It is put thus: "He trusted on the LORD that he would deliver him: let him deliver him"; "Do not come to us with your fiddle-faddle about God's helping all his chosen. Here is a man who is one of his people, will he help him? Do not talk to us big things about Jehovah at the Red Sea, or in the Desert of Sinai, or God helping his people in ages past. Here is a living man before us who trusted in God that he would deliver him: let him deliver him now." You know how Satan will pick out one of the most afflicted, and pointing his fingers at him will cry, "Let him deliver HIM." Brethren, the test is fair. God will be true to every believer. If any one child of God could be lost, it would be quite enough to enable the devil to spoil all the glory of God for ever. If one promise of God to one of his people should fail, that one failure would suffice to mar the veracity of the Lord to all eternity; they would publish it in the "Diabolical Gazette," and in every street of Tophet[10] they would howl it out, "God has failed. God has broken his promise. God has ceased to be faithful to his people." It would then be a horrible reproach—"He trusted in God to deliver him, but he did not deliver him."

A Christian man may be beaten in business, he may fail to meet all demands, and then Satan yells, "Let him deliver him now." The poor man has been out of work for two or three months, tramping the streets of London until he has worn out his boots; he has been brought to his last penny. I think I hear the laugh of the Prince of Darkness as he cries, "Let him deliver him now." Or else the believer is very ill in body, and low in spirit, and then Satan howls, "Let him deliver him now." Some of us have been in very trying positions. We were moved

10. Tophet is a Middle English term for hell.

with indignation because of deadly error, and we spoke plainly, but men refused to hear. Those we relied upon deserted us; good men sought their own ease and would not march with us, and we had to bear testimony for despised truth alone, until we were ourselves despised. Then the adversary shouted, "Let him deliver him now." Be it so! We do not refuse the test. Our God whom we serve will deliver us. We will not bow down to modern thought nor worship the image which human wisdom has set up. Our God is God both of hills and of valleys. He will not fail his servants, albeit that for a while he forbears that he may try their faith. We dare accept the test, and say, "Let him deliver us now."

But God's ways of deliverance are his own. He does not deliver according to the translation put upon "deliverance" by the ribald throng. He does not deliver according to the interpretation put upon "deliverance" by our shrinking flesh and blood. He delivers, but it is in his own way. Let me remark that, if God delivers you and me in the same way as he delivered his own Son, we can have no cause of complaint. If the deliverance which he vouchsafed to us is of the same kind as that which he vouchsafed to the Only Begotten, we may well be content. Well, what kind of a deliverance was that? Did the Father tear up the cross from the earth? Did he proceed to draw out the nails from the sacred hands and feet of his dear Son? Did he set him down upon that "green hill far away, beyond the city wall," and place in his hand a sword of fire with which to smite his adversaries? Did he bid the earth open and swallow up all his foes? No; nothing of the kind.

Jehovah did not interpose to spare his Son a single pang; but he let him die. He let him be taken as a dead man down from the cross and laid in a tomb. Jesus went through with his suffering to the bitter end. O brothers and sisters, this may be God's way of delivering us. We have trusted in God that he would deliver us; and his rendering of his promise is, that he will enable us to go through with it; we shall suffer to the last, and triumph in so doing.

Yet God's way of delivering those who trust in him is always the best way. If the Father had taken his Son down from the cross, what would have been the result? Redemption unaccomplished, salvation work undone, and Jesus returning with his lifework unfinished. This would not have been deliverance, but defeat. It was much better for our Lord Jesus to die. Now he has paid the ransom for his elect, and having accomplished the great purpose of atonement, he has slept a while in the heart of the earth, and now has ascended to his throne in the endless glories of heaven. It was deliverance of the fullest kind; for from the pangs of his death has come the joy of life to his redeemed. It is not God's will that every mountain should be leveled, but that we should be the stronger for climbing the Hill Difficulty. God will deliver; he must deliver, but he will do it in our cases, as in the case of our Lord, in the best possible manner.

Day 19

The Three Hours' Darkness

Now from the sixth hour there was darkness
over all the land until the ninth hour.
Matthew 27:45

Never forget that this miracle of the closing of the eye of day at high noon was performed by our Lord in his weakness. He had walked the sea, and raised the dead, and healed the sick, in the days of his strength; but now he has come to his lowest, the fever is on him, he is faint and thirsty. He hangs on the borders of dissolution; yet has he power to darken the sun at noon. He is still very God of very God. If he can do this in his weakness, what is he not able to do in his strength?

This darkness teaches us what Jesus suffered: It aids us to guess at the griefs which we may not actually see. The darkness is the symbol of the wrath of God which fell on those who slew his only begotten Son. God was angry, and his frown removed the light of day. Well might he be angry, when sin was murdering his only Son; when the Jewish husbandmen were saying, "This is the heir. Come, let us kill him and have his inheritance" (Matthew 21:38). This is God's wrath towards all mankind, for practically all men concurred in the death of Jesus. That wrath has brought men into darkness; they are ignorant, blinded, bewildered. They have come to love darkness better than light because their deeds are evil. In that darkness they do not repent, but go on to reject the Christ of God. Into this darkness God cannot look upon them in complacency; but he views them as children of darkness, and heirs of wrath, for whom is reserved the blackness of darkness forever.

The symbol also tells us what our Lord Jesus Christ endured. The darkness outside of him was the figure of the darkness that was within him. In Gethsemane a thick darkness fell upon our Lord's spirit. He was "very sorrowful, even to death" (Matthew 26:38). His joy was communion with God—that joy was gone, and he was in the dark. His day was the light of his Father's face: that face was hidden and a terrible night gathered around him. Brothers, I should sin against that veil if I were to pretend that I could tell you what the sorrow was which oppressed the Savior's soul: Only so far can I speak as it has been given me to have fellowship with him in his sufferings. Have you ever felt a deep and overwhelming horror of sin—your own sin and the sins of others? Have you ever seen sin in the light of God's love? Has it ever darkly hovered over your sensitive conscience? Has an unknown sense of wrath crept over you like midnight gloom; and has it been about you, around you, above you, and within you? Have you felt shut up in your feebleness, and yet shut out from God? Have you looked around and found no help, no comfort even in God—no hope, no peace? In all this you have sipped a little of that salt sea into which our Lord was cast. If, like Abraham, you have felt a horror of great darkness creep over you, then have you had a taste of what your divine Lord suffered when it pleased the Father to bruise him and to put him to grief (Isaiah 53:10).

This it was that made him sweat great drops of blood falling to the ground; and this it was which on the cross made him utter that appalling cry, "My God, my God, why have you forsaken me?" (Mark 15:34). It was not the crown of thorns, or the scourge, or the cross which made him cry, but the darkness, the awful darkness of desertion which oppressed his mind and made him feel like one distraught. All that could comfort him was withdrawn, and all that could distress him was piled upon him. "The spirit of a man will sustain his infirmity; but a wounded spirit who can bear?" (Proverbs 18:14 KJV). Our Savior's spirit was wounded, and he cried, "My heart is like wax; it is melted within my breast" (Psalm 22:14). Of all natural and spiritual comfort he was bereft, and his distress was utter and entire. The darkness of Calvary did not, like an ordinary night, reveal the stars; but it darkened every lamp of heaven. His strong crying and tears denoted the deep sorrow of his soul. He bore all it was possible for his capacious mind to bear, though enlarged and invigorated by union with the Godhead. He bore the equivalent of hell; nay, not that only, but he bore that which stood instead of ten thousand hells so far as the vindication of the law is concerned. Our Lord rendered in his death agony a homage to justice far greater than if a world had been doomed to destruction. When I have said that, what more can I say? Well may I tell you that this unutterable darkness, this hiding of the divine face, expresses more of the woes of Jesus than words can ever tell.

Again, I think I see in that darkness, also what it was that Jesus was battling with, for we must never forget that the cross was a battlefield to him, wherein he triumphed gloriously. He was fighting then with darkness; with the powers of darkness of which Satan is the head; with the darkness of human ignorance, depravity, and falsehood.

The battle thus apparent at Golgotha has been raging ever since. Then was the conflict at its height; for the chiefs of the two great armies met in personal conflict. The present battle in which you and I take our little share is as nothing compared with that wherein all the powers of darkness in their dense battalions hurled themselves against the Almighty Son of God. He bore their onset, endured the tremendous shock of their assault, and in the end, with shout of victory, he led captivity captive. He by his power and Godhead turned midnight into day again, and brought back to this world a reign of light which, blessed be God, shall never come to a close. Come to battle again, you hosts of darkness, if you dare! The cross has defeated you: the cross shall defeat you. Hallelujah! The cross is the ensign of victory; its light is the death of darkness. The cross is the lighthouse which guides poor weather-beaten humanity into the harbor of peace: This is the lamp which shines over the door of the great Father's house to lead his prodigals home.

Let us not be afraid of all the darkness which besets us on our way home, since Jesus is the light which conquers it all. Brethren, no light will ever come to dark hearts unless Jesus shall speak; and the light will not be clear until we hear the voice of his sorrows on our behalf, as he cries, "Why have you forsaken me?" His voice of grief must be the end of our griefs: His cry out of the darkness must cheer away our gloom, and bring the heavenly morning to our minds.

Day 20

The Saddest Cry from the Cross

And about the ninth hour Jesus cried out with a loud voice, saying, "Eli, Eli, lema sabachthani?" that is, "My God, my God, why have you forsaken me?"
Matthew 27:46

I think I can understand the words, "My God, my God, why have you forsaken me?" as they are written by David in the twenty-second Psalm; but the same words, "My God, my God, why have you forsaken me?" when uttered by Jesus on the cross, I cannot comprehend, so I shall not pretend to be able to explain them. There is no plummet that can fathom this deep; there is no eagle's eye that can penetrate the mystery that surrounds this strange question. I feel more like one who has looked into a deep mine—or like one who has been part of the way down, and shuddered as he passed through the murky darkness but who would not dare to go much lower. For this cry, "Eli, Eli, lema sabachthani?" is a tremendous deep; no man will ever be able to fathom it.

Jesus was accustomed to address God as his Father. If you turn to his many prayers, you will find him almost invariably—if not invariably—speaking to God as his Father. And, truly, he stands in that relationship both as God and as man. Yet, in this instance, he does not say, "Father;" but "My God, my God." Was it that he had any doubt about his sonship? Assuredly not; Satan had assailed him in the wilderness with the insinuation, "If you are the Son of God," but Christ had put him to the rout; and I feel persuaded that Satan had not gained any advantage over him, even on the cross, which could have made him doubt whether he was the Son of God or not.

I think that our Savior was speaking then as man, and that this is the reason why he cried, "My God, my God," rather than "My Father." I think he must have been speaking as man; as I can scarcely bring my mind to the point of conceiving that God the Son could say to God the Father, "My God, my God." There is such a wonderful blending of the human and the Divine in the person of the Lord Jesus Christ that, though it may not be absolutely accurate to ascribe to the Deity some things in the life of Christ, yet is he so completely God and man that, often, Scripture does speak of things that must belong to the humanity only as if they belonged to the Godhead. For instance, in his charge to the Ephesian elders, the apostle Paul said, "care for the church of God, which he obtained with his own blood" (Acts 20:28)—an incorrect expression, if judged according to the rule of the logician; but accurate enough according to the scriptural method of using words in their proper sense. Yet I do think that we must draw a distinction between the Divinity and the humanity here. As the Lord Jesus said, "My God, my God," it was because it was his humanity that was mainly to be considered just then.

And O my brethren, does it not show us what a real man, the Christ of God was, that he could be forsaken of his God? We might have supposed that, Christ being Emmanuel—God with us—the Godhead and the manhood being indissolubly united in one person, it would have been impossible for him to be forsaken of God. We might also have inferred, for the same reason, that it would have been impossible for him to have been scourged, and spit upon, and especially that it would not have been possible for him to die. Yet all these things were made, not only possible, but also sacredly certain. In order to complete the redemption of his chosen people, it was necessary for him to be both God's well-beloved Son, and to be forsaken of his Father; he could truly say, as his saints also have sometimes had to say, "My God, my God, why have you forsaken me!" Persecuted and forsaken believer, behold your Brother in adversity!

But what was this forsaking? We are trying to come a little closer to this burning yet unconsumed bush—with our shoes off our feet, I hope, all the while—and in this spirit we ask, "What was this forsaking?" Christ made no mistake about this matter, for God had forsaken him. It was really so. When he said, "Why have you forsaken me?" he spoke infallible truth, and his mind was under no cloud whatsoever. He knew what he was saying, and he was right in what he said, for his Father had forsaken him for the time.

What, then, can this expression mean? Does it mean that God did not love his Son? O beloved, let us, with the utmost detestation, fling away any suspicion of the kind that we may have harbored! God did forsake his Son, but he loved him as much when he forsook him as at any other period. I even venture to say that, if it had been possible for God's love towards his Son to be increased, he would have delighted in him more when he was standing as the suffering representative of his chosen people than ever he had delighted in him before. We do not indulge, for a single moment, the thought that God was angry with him personally, or looked upon him as unworthy of his love, or regarded him as one upon whom he could not smile, because of anything displeasing in himself; yet the fact remains that God had forsaken him, for Christ was under no mistake about that matter. He rightly felt that his Father had withdrawn the comfortable light of his countenance, that he had, for the time being, lost the sense of his Father's favor—not the favor itself, but the consciousness of that divine aid and succor which he had formerly enjoyed—so he felt himself like a man left all alone; and he was not only left all alone by his friends, but also by his God.

After all, beloved, the only solution of the mystery is this, Jesus Christ was forsaken of God because we deserved to be forsaken of God. He was there, on the cross, in our room, and place, and stead; and as the sinner, by reason of his sin deserves not to enjoy the favor of God, so Jesus Christ, standing in the place of the sinner, and enduring that which would vindicate the justice of God, had to come under the cloud, as the sinner must have come, if Christ had not taken his place. But, then, since he has come under it, let us recollect that he was thus left of God that you and I, who believe in him, might never be left of God. Since he, for a little while, was separated from his Father, we may boldly cry, "Who shall separate us from the love of Christ?" (Romans 8:35) and, with the apostle Paul, we may confidently affirm that nothing in the whole universe shall be able to separate us from the love of God, which is in Christ Jesus our Lord (Romans 8:39).

Day 21
It Is Finished

"It is finished."
John 19:30

It is the language of a Savior. Our Lord's mission to our world was simply and singly to save. He came for no other object than to save man, to give his life a ransom for many; To provide, to execute an expedient devised in the eternal council, and purpose, and love of the triune God, for securing the full redemption of his church—an expedient that should harmonize and unite all the moral attributes and perfections of his being and then lower from the battlement of heaven to sin's fathomless depths the golden chain of mercy, pardoning mercy, to which, if in faith you take hold, it will lift you up to the throne from whence it came.

It is the fashion of the present day to ignore the Saviorship of Jesus, and to represent his person, and his life, and his death in any and every form, rather than acknowledge that he died on the cross in the character of a Savior, and that faith in the merits of his obedience and love for the efficacy of his death, constitutes the only basis on which a lost sinner can build his hope of heaven. I ask you, my beloved hearers, what is the grand object of modern heresy but to undermine the cross of Christ, to ignore the sacrifice of his death, to blot out the glorious atonement, and to reduce the splendid paraphernalia of Calvary, with all its moral and sublime results, to a mere nonentity?

His death, his obedience was the obedience of the law-maker in the form of the law-fulfiller to a law which man had broken and violated, and that obedience perfect and complete, so that broken law is the righteousness that justifies the ungodly and places him that believes spotless before God. Hold you fast that truth—the imputed righteousness of the Lord our righteousness wrought and complete in his perfect obedience to the precepts of a broken law. His death on Calvary was an atonement to divine justice; the shedding of his blood was for the remission of man's sins; the paying out of his soul to death was the perfect honor given to the moral government of Jehovah; and when he went out of the streets of Jerusalem staggering beneath the beam on which he was to be impaled; when, with lowly footsteps, he ascended that sacred hill Calvary; when there, like a lamb led to the slaughter, he gave himself up uncomplainingly, unreservedly into the hands of the executioners; when they stretched him on that tree, transfixed his limbs to those beams, lifted it and let it fall into the place excavated for it to stand in; when there he poured out his holy soul unto death—oh, my brethren, it was to harmonize justice and mercy, holiness and truth, to blend in one vast bow of hope all these divine attributes, that they might span the moral heaven and encircle our lost humanity. It was then he gave up his soul unto death, and offered up that sacrifice for sin, which man, in his madness, folly, and infidelity, dares in this our day to ignore and to deny.

Yes, it is the language of a Savior. Those words speak hope to the hopeless, pardon to the guilty, acceptance to the lost; they tell you, O poor sin-smitten, burdened sinner, that there is hope, pardon even for you. He had finished all that justice asked that the law demanded, he had finished the mission his Father had confided to his hands, he had finished the grand oblation that has to restore to God's moral government the glory it had lost in man's apostacy. He had finished all the ancient types, predictions, and shadows; he tore the veil in two and opened the bright pathway for the sinner to retrace his steps back to paradise, back to God, and once more feel the warm embrace of his Father's forgiving love.

Oh! it is the language of a Savior which bids you come. Poor broken-hearted sinner, with all your burden of sin, believe and be saved! It bids you come without money and without price; it tells you the blood he poured from his broken heart can wash out and cancel the deepest stain that is on your soul; it tells you there is room in that bosom which he laid bare to the lightening stroke of God's wrath; it tells you, dry your tears, embrace the cross, trust in the finished work of Christ; fling to the heavens all your own righteousness, enwrap you up by faith in the righteousness of Christ, and all the minstrelsy of heaven shall tune their harps of gold, and make the heavens reverberate with their songs of praise over your submission in faith to the atonement of the Son of God.

But this is also the shout of a conqueror. Christ was a man of war, our glorious Joshua was he; he had come to gird on the sword, to invest him with the armor, and to go out and battle with Satan, with sin, and with hell. It was a terrible conflict, it was a fearful battle, but he girded himself for the mighty and the solemn work, and he completed it, he finished it. He met his foes on the battle field, confronted all his enemies, and on the cross he destroyed—he divested death of its sting, triumphed over Satan, the grave, and hell, and as he expired exclaimed, "It is finished!" Oh what a sublime conflict was that, my brethren, when the Captain of our salvation met single-handed and overcame the powers of darkness, fought the fight, won the victory, and died, saying "It is finished!"

What a spring of comfort flows from it to the true believer amid his innumerable failures, flaws, and imperfections. What service do you perform, what duty do you discharge of which you can say, "It is finished?" Alas! not one; your service is imperfect, your obedience is incomplete, your love is fluctuating, yea, upon it all are visible the marks of human defilement and defect.

But here is the work which God most delights in, "finished." "You are complete in Him" (Colossians 2:10 NKJV). Turn you, then, your eye of faith out of yourself, and off all your own doings, and deal more immediately, closely, and obediently with the finished work of Immanuel. Come away from your fickle love, from your weak faith, from your little fruitfulness, from your uneven walk, from all your shortcomings and imperfections, and let your eye of faith repose where God's eye of complacent love reposes, on the finished work of Jesus. God beholds you only in Christ—it is not upon you he looks, but on his beloved Son, and upon you in him, "by which He made us accepted in the Beloved" (Ephesians 1:6 NKJV).

Day 22

Our Lord's Last Cry from the Cross

Then Jesus, calling out with a loud voice, said,
"Father, into your hands I commit my spirit!"
And having said this he breathed his last.
Luke 23:46

Do you see our Lord? He is dying; and as yet, his face is toward man. His last word to man is the cry, "It is finished." Hear, all you sons of men, he speaks to you, "It is finished." Could you have a choicer word with which he should say "Adieu" to you in the hour of death? He tells you not to fear that his work is imperfect, not to tremble lest it should prove insufficient. He speaks to you, and declares with his dying utterance, "It is finished."

Now he has done with you, and he turns his face the other way. His day's work is done, his more than Herculean toil is accomplished, and the great Champion is going back to his Father's throne, and he speaks; but not to you. His last word is addressed to his Father, "Father, into your hands I commend my spirit." These are his first words in going home to his Father, as "It is finished," is his last word as, for a while, he quits our company. Think of these words, and may they be your first words, too, when you return to your Father! May you speak thus to your Divine Father in the hour of death!

What is the doctrine of this last word of our Lord Jesus Christ? God is his Father, and God is our Father. He who himself said, "Father," did not say for himself, "Our Father," for the Father is Christ's Father in a higher sense than he is ours; but yet he is not more truly the Father of Christ than he is our Father if we have believed in Jesus. "For in Christ Jesus you are all sons of God, through faith" (Galatians 3:26). Jesus said to Mary Magdalene, "I am ascending to my Father, and your Father, to my God and your God" (John 20:17).

Believe the doctrine of the fatherhood of God to his people.

As I have warned you before, abhor the doctrine of the universal fatherhood of God, for it is a lie, and a deep deception. It stabs at the heart, first, of the doctrine of the adoption, which is taught in Scripture, for how can God adopt men if they are all his children already? In the second place, it stabs at the heart of the doctrine of regeneration, which is certainly taught in the Word of God. Now, it is by regeneration and faith that we become the children of God, but how can that be if we are the children of God already? "But to all who did receive him, who believed in his name, he gave the right to become children of God who were born, not of blood nor of the will of the flesh nor of the will of man, but of God" (John 1:12–13). How can God give to men the power to become his sons if they have it already? Believe not that lie of the devil, but believe this truth of God, that Christ and all who are by living faith in Christ may rejoice in the fatherhood of God.

Next learn this doctrine, that in this fact lies our chief comfort. In our hour of trouble, in our time of warfare, let us say, "Father." You notice that the first cry from the cross is like the last; the highest note is like the lowest. Jesus begins with, "Father, forgive them," and he finishes with, "Father, into your hands I commit my spirit." To help you in a stern duty like forgiveness, cry, "Father." To help you in sore suffering and death, cry, "Father." Your main strength lies in your being truly a child of God.

Let us enjoy the high privilege of resting in God in all times of danger and pain. The doctor has just told you that you will have to undergo an operation. Say, "Father, into your hands I commit my spirit." There is every probability that that weakness of yours, or that disease of yours, will increase upon you, and that by-and-by you will have to take to your bed, and lie there perhaps for many a day. Then say, "Father, into your hands I commit my spirit." Do not fret; for that will not help you. Do not fear the future; for that will not aid you. Give yourself up (it is your privilege to do so) to the keeping of those dear hands that were pierced for you, to the love of that dear heart which was ruptured with the spear to purchase your redemption. It is wonderful what rest of spirit God can give to a man or a woman in the very worst condition.

Learn the next doctrine, that dying is going home to our Father. I said to an old friend, not long ago, "Old Mr. So-and-so has gone home." I meant that he was dead. He said, "Yes, where else should he go?" I thought that was a wise question. Where else should we go? When we grow grey, and our day's work is done, where should we go but home? So, when Christ has said, "It is finished," his next word, of course, is "Father." He has finished his earthly course, and now he will go home to heaven. Just as a child runs to its mother's bosom when it is tired, and wants to fall asleep, so Christ says, "Father," before he falls asleep in death.

Learn another doctrine, that if God is our Father, and we regard ourselves as going home when we die, because we go to him, then he will receive us. There is no hint that we can commit our spirit to God, and yet that God will not have us. Remember how Stephen, beneath a shower of stones, cried, "Lord Jesus, receive my spirit" (Acts 7:59). Let us, however we may die, make this our last emotion if not our last expression, "Father, receive my spirit." Shall not our heavenly Father receive his children? If you, being evil, receive your children at nightfall, when they come home to sleep, shall not your Father, who is in heaven, receive you when your day's work is done? That is the doctrine we are to learn from this last cry from the cross, the fatherhood of God and all that comes of it to believers.

Day 23
The Rent Veil

And behold, the curtain of the temple was torn in two, from top to bottom.
Matthew 27:51

In actual historical fact the glorious veil of the temple has been torn in two from the top to the bottom: as a matter of spiritual fact, which is far more important to us, the separating legal ordinance is abolished. There was under the law this ordinance—that no man should ever go into the holiest of all, with the one exception of the high priest, and he but once in the year, and not without blood. If any man had attempted to enter there he must have died, as guilty of great presumption and of profane intrusion into the secret place of the Most High. Who could stand in the presence of Him who is a consuming fire (Hebrews 12:29)? This ordinance of distance runs all through the law; for even the holy place, which was the vestibule of the holy of holies, was for the priests alone. The place of the people was one of distance. At the very first institution of the law when God descended upon Sinai, the ordinance was, "And you shall set limits for the people all around" (Exodus 19:12). There was no invitation to draw near.

All this is ended. The precept to keep back is abrogated, and the invitation is, "Come to me, all who labor and are heavy laden" (Matthew 11:28). "Let us draw near" (Hebrews 10:22) is now the filial spirit of the gospel. How thankful I am for this! What a joy it is to my soul! My brother, no veil remains. Why do you stand afar off, and tremble like a slave? Draw near with full assurance of faith. The veil is rent; access is free. Come boldly to the throne of grace (Hebrews 4:16).

This rending of the veil signified, also, the removal of the separating sin. Sin is, after all, the great divider between God and man. That veil of blue and purple and fine twined linen could not really separate man from God: For he is, as to his omnipresence, not far from any one of us. Sin is a far more effectual wall of separation; it opens an abyss between the sinner and his Judge. Sin shuts out prayer, and praise, and every form of religious exercise. Sin makes God walk contrary to us, because we walk contrary to him. Sin, by separating the soul from God, causes spiritual death, which is both the effect and the penalty of transgression. How can two walk together except they be agreed (Amos 3:3)? How can a holy God have fellowship with unholy creatures? Shall justice dwell with injustice? Shall perfect purity abide with the abominations of evil? No, it cannot be.

Our Lord Jesus Christ put away sin by the sacrifice of himself. He takes away the sin of the world, and so the veil is rent. By the shedding of his most precious blood we are cleansed from all sin, and that most gracious promise of the new covenant is fulfilled—"I will remember their sins no more" (Hebrews 8:12).

For believers the veil is not rolled up, but rent. The veil was not unhooked, and carefully folded up, and put away, so that it might be put in its place at some future time. Oh, no! But the divine hand took it and rent it top to bottom. It can never be hung up again; that is impossible. Between those who are in Christ Jesus and the great God, there will never be another separation. "Who shall separate us from the love of Christ?" (Romans 8:35). Only one veil was made, and as that is rent, the one and only separator is destroyed. I delight to think of this. The devil himself can never divide me from God now. He may and will attempt to shut me out from God; but the worst he could do would be to hang up a rent veil. What would that avail but to exhibit his impotence? God has rent the veil, and the devil cannot mend it.

There is access between a believer and his God; and there must be such free access forever, since the veil is not rolled up, and put on one side to be hung up again in days to come; but it is rent, and rendered useless. The rent is not in one corner, but in the midst, as Luke tells us. It is not a slight rent through which we may see a little; but it is rent from the top to the bottom. There is an entrance made for the greatest sinners. If there had only been a small hole cut through it, the lesser offenders might have crept through; but what an act of abounding mercy is this, that the veil is rent in the midst, and rent from top to bottom, so that the chief of sinners may find ample passage! This also shows that for believers there is no hindrance to the fullest and freest access to God. Oh, for much boldness, this morning, to come where God has not only set open the door, but has lifted the door from its hinges; yea, removed it, post, and bar, and all!

I want you to notice that this veil, when it was rent, was rent by God, not by man. It was not the act of an irreverent mob; it was not the midnight outrage of a set of profane priests; it was the act of God alone. Nobody stood within the veil; and on the outer side of it stood the priests only fulfilling their ordinary vocation of offering sacrifice. It must have astounded them when they saw that holy place laid bare in a moment. How they fled, as they saw that massive veil divided without human hand in a second of time! Who rent it? Who but God himself? If another had done it, there might have been a mistake about it, and the mistake might need to be remedied by replacing the curtain; but if the Lord has done it, it is done rightly, it is done finally, it is done irreversibly. It is God himself who has laid sin on Christ, and in Christ has put that sin away. God himself has opened the gate of heaven to believers, and cast up a highway along which the souls of men may travel to himself. God himself has set the ladder between earth and heaven. Come to him now, humble ones. Behold, he sets before you an open door!

Day 24

The Miracles of Our Lord's Death

And the earth shook, and the rocks were split. The tombs also were opened. And many bodies of the saints who had fallen asleep were raised, and coming out of the tombs after his resurrection they went into the holy city and appeared to many.
Matthew 27:51–53

These wonders accumulate, and they depend upon each other. The quaking earth produced, no doubt, the rending of the rocks; and the rending of the rocks aided in the fourth wonder: The graves opened, and the dead revived. It is the great consequence of the death of Christ. The graves were opened.

I think we have in this last miracle "the history of a man." There he lies dead—corrupt, dead in trespasses and sins. But what a beautiful sepulcher he lies in! He is a churchgoer; he is a dissenter—whichever you please of the two; he is a very moral person; he is a gentleman; he is a citizen; he is Master of his company; he will be Lord Mayor one day; he is so good—oh, he is so good! Yet he has no grace in his heart, no Christ in his faith, no love to God. You see what a sepulcher he lies in—a dead soul in a gilded tomb. By his cross our Lord splits this sepulcher and destroys it. What are our merits worth in the presence of the cross? The death of Christ is the death of self-righteousness. Jesus's death is a superfluity if we can save ourselves. If we are so good that we do not want the Savior, why, then, did Jesus bleed his life away upon the tree? The cross breaks up the sepulchers of hypocrisy, formalism, and self-righteousness in which the spiritually dead are hidden away.

What next? It opens the graves. The earth springs apart. There lies the dead man; he is revealed to the light. The cross of Christ does that! The man is not yet made alive by grace, but he is discovered to himself. He knows that he lies in the grave of his sin. He has sufficient of the power of God upon him to make him lie, not like a corpse covered up with marble, but like a corpse from which the gravedigger has flung away the sods, and left it naked to the light of day. Oh, it is a grand thing when the cross thus opens the graves! You cannot convince men of sin except by the preaching of a crucified Savior. The lance with which we reach the hearts of men is that same lance which pierced the Savior's heart. We have to use the crucifixion as the means of crucifying self-righteousness, and making the man confess that he is dead in sin.

After the sepulchers had been broken up, and the graves had been opened, what followed next? Life was imparted. "Many bodies of the saints who had fallen asleep were raised." They had turned to dust; but when you have a miracle you may as well have a great one. I wonder that people, when they can believe one miracle, make any difficulty of another. Introduce omnipotence, and difficulties have ceased. So in this miracle. The bodies came together on a sudden, and there they were, complete and ready for the rising. What a wonderful thing is the implantation of life!

I will not speak of it in a dead man, but I would speak of it in a dead heart. O God, send your life into some dead heart at this moment while I speak! That which brings life into dead souls is the death of Jesus. While we behold the atonement, and view our Lord bleeding in our stead, the divine Spirit works upon the man, and life is breathed into him. He takes away the heart of stone, and gives a heart of flesh that palpitates with a new life. This is the wondrous work of the cross: It is by the death of our Lord that regeneration comes to men. There were no new births if it were not for that one death. If Jesus had not died, we had remained dead. If he had not bowed his head, none of us could have lifted up our heads. If he had not there on the cross passed from among the living, we must have remained among the dead forever and forever.

Now pass on, and you will see that those persons who received life, in due time quitted their graves. It is written that they came out of their graves. Of course they did. What living men would wish to stay in their graves? And you, my dear hearers, if the Lord quickens you, will not stay in your graves. If you have been accustomed to strong drink, or to any other besetting sin, you will quit it; you will not feel any attachment to your sepulcher. If you have lived in ungodly company, and found amusement in questionable places, you will not stop in your graves. We shall not have need to come after you to lead you away from your old associations. You will be eager to get out of them. If any person here should be buried alive, and if he should be discovered in his coffin before he had breathed his last, I am sure that, if the sod were lifted, and the lid were taken off, he would not need prayerful entreaties to come out of his grave. Far from it. Life loves not the prison of death. So may God grant that the dying Savior may fetch you out of the graves in which you are still living; and, if he now quickens you, I am sure that the death of our Lord will make you reckon that if one died for all, then all died, and that he died for all, that they which live should not live henceforth unto themselves, but unto him that died for them and rose again (2 Corinthians 5:14–15).

Which way did these people go after they had come out of their graves? We are told that "they went into the holy city." Exactly so. And he that has felt the power of the cross may well make the best of his way to holiness. He will long to join himself with God's people; he will wish to go up to God's house, and to have fellowship with the thrice-holy God. I should not expect that quickened ones would go anywhere else. Every creature goes to its own company, the beast to its lair, and the bird to its nest; and the restored and regenerated man makes his way to the holy city. Does not the cross draw us to the church of God? I would not wish one to join the church from any motive that is not fetched from the five wounds and bleeding side of Jesus. We give ourselves first to Christ, and then to his people for his dear sake. It is the cross that does it.

We are told—to close this marvelous story—that they went into the holy city "and appeared unto many." What does this teach us, but that, if the Lord's grace should raise us from the dead, we must take care to show it? Let us appear unto many. Let the life that God has given us be manifest. Let us not hide it, but let us go to our former friends and make our epiphanies as Christ made his. For his glory's sake let us have our manifestation and appearance unto others. Glory be to the dying Savior! All praise to the great Sacrifice!

Day 25

Mourning at the Sight of the Crucified

And all the crowds that had assembled for this spectacle, when they saw what had taken place, returned home beating their breasts.
Luke 23:48

They all smote their breasts, but not all from the same cause. They were all afraid, not all from the same reason. The outward manifestations were alike in the whole mass, but the grades of difference in feeling were as many as the minds in which they ruled.

There were many, no doubt, who were merely moved with a transient emotion. They had seen the death agonies of a remarkable man, and the attendant wonders had persuaded them that he was something more than an ordinary being, and therefore, they were afraid. With a kind of indefinite fear, grounded upon no very intelligent reasoning, they were alarmed, because God was angry, and had closed the eye of day upon them, and made the rocks to rend; and, burdened with this indistinct fear, they went their way trembling and humbled to their several homes; but peradventure, before the next morning light had dawned, they had forgotten it all, and the next day found them greedy for another bloody spectacle, and ready to nail another Christ to the cross, if there had been such another to be found in the land. Their beating of the breast was not a breaking of the heart.

How often in the preaching of the cross has this been the only result in tens of thousands! In this house, where so many souls have been converted, many more have shed tears which have been wiped away, and the reason of their tears has been forgotten. A handkerchief has dried up their emotions. Alas! Alas! Alas! that while it may be difficult to move men with the story of the cross to weeping, it is even more difficult to make those emotions permanent. "I have seen something wonderful this morning," said one who had listened to a faithful and earnest preacher, "I have seen a whole congregation in tears." "Alas!" said the preacher, "there is something more wonderful still, for most of them will go their way to forget that they ever shed a tear." Ah, my hearers, shall it be always so—always so? By the love you bear your souls, I pray you escape from the wrath to come!

Others amongst that great crowd exhibited emotion based upon more thoughtful reflection. They saw that they had shared in the murder of an innocent person. "Alas!" said they, "we see through it all now. That man was no offender. In all that we have ever heard or seen of him, he did good, and only good: he always healed the sick, fed the hungry, and raised the dead. There is not a word of all his teaching that is really contrary to the law of God. He was a pure and holy man. We have all been duped. Those priests have egged us on to put to death one whom it were a thousand mercies if we could restore to life again at once. Our race has killed its benefactor." Such feelings would abide, but I can suppose that they might not bring men to sincere repentance; for while they might feel sorry that they had oppressed the innocent, yet, perceiving nothing more in Jesus than mere mistreated virtue and suffering manhood, the natural emotion might soon pass away, and the moral and spiritual result be of no great value.

How frequently have we seen in our hearers that same description of emotion! They have regretted that Christ should be put to death, they have felt like that old king of France, who said, "I wish I had been there with ten thousand of my soldiers, I would have cut their throats sooner than they should have touched him;" but those very feelings have been evidence that they did not feel their share in the guilt as they ought to have done, and that to them the cross of Jesus was no more a saving spectacle than the death of a common martyr. Dear hearers, beware of making the cross to be a commonplace thing with you. Look beyond the sufferings of the innocent manhood of Jesus, and see upon the tree the atoning sacrifice of Christ, or else you look to the cross in vain.

No doubt there were a few in the crowd who smote upon their breasts because they felt, "We have put to death a prophet of God. As of old, our nation slew Isaiah, and put to death others of the Master's servants, so today they have nailed to the cross one of the last of the Prophets, and his blood will be upon us and upon our children." Peradventure some of them said, "This man claimed to be Messiah, and the miracles which attended his death prove that he was so. His life betokens it and his death declares it. What will become of our nation if we have slain the Prince of Peace! How will God visit us if we have put his prophet to death!" Such mourning was in advance of other forms; it showed a deeper thought and a clearer knowledge, and it may have been an admirable preparation for the after hearing of the gospel; but it would not of itself suffice as evidence of grace.

I shall be glad if my hearers in this house today are persuaded by the character of Christ that he must have been a prophet sent of God, and that he was the Messiah promised of old; and I shall be gratified if they, therefore, lament the shameful cruelties which he received from our apostate race. Such emotions of compunction and pity are most commendable, and under God's blessing they may prove to be the furrows of your heart in which the gospel may take root.

In the motley company who all went home smiting on their breasts, let us hope that there were some who said, "Truly this man was the Son of God" (Mark 15:39), and mourned to think he should have suffered for their transgressions, and been put to grief for their iniquities. Those who came to that point were saved. Blessed were the eyes that looked upon the slaughtered Lamb in such a way as that, and happy were the hearts that there and then were broken because he was bruised and put to grief for their sakes.

Beloved, aspire to this. May God's grace bring you to see in Jesus Christ no other than God made flesh, hanging upon the tree in agony, to die, the just for the unjust, that we may be saved. O come and repose your trust in him, and then smite upon your breasts at the thought that such a victim should have been necessary for your redemption; then may you cease to smite your breasts, and begin to clap your hands for very joy; for they who thus bewail a Savior may rejoice in him, for he is theirs and they are his.

Day 26
On the Cross After Death

For these things took place that the Scripture might be fulfilled: "Not one of his bones will be broken." And again another Scripture says, "They will look on him whom they have pierced."
John 19:36–37

Two things are predicted: not a bone of him must be broken, and he must be pierced. These were the Scriptures which now remained to be accomplished. I want you to notice concerning this case, that it was singularly complicated. It was negative and positive: the Savior's bones must not be broken, and he must be pierced. In the type of the Passover lamb it was expressly enacted that not a bone of it should be broken (Exodus 12:46); therefore not a bone of Jesus must be broken. At the same time, according to Zechariah 12:10, the Lord must be pierced. He must not only be pierced with the nails, and so fulfill the prophecy, "They pierced my hands and my feet;" but he must be conspicuously pierced, so that he can be emphatically regarded as a pierced one. How were these prophecies, and a multitude more, to be accomplished? Only God himself could have brought to pass the fulfillment of prophecies which were of all kinds, and appeared to be confused, and even in contradiction to each other.

The fulfillment of these two prophecies was especially improbable. It did not seem at all likely that when the order was given to break the legs of the crucified, Roman soldiers would abstain from the deed. How could the body of Christ be preserved after such an order had been issued? Those four soldiers are evidently determined to carry out the governor's orders. Roman soldiers are apt to fulfill their commissions very literally, and they are not often moved with much desire to avoid barbarities. Can you see them intent upon their errand? Will they not even now mangle that sacred body? The ordinary Roman soldier was so used to deeds of slaughter, so accustomed to an empire which had been established with blood and iron, that the idea of pity never crossed his soul, except to be scouted as a womanly feeling unworthy of a brave man. Yet behold and wonder! The order is given to break their legs: Two out of the three have suffered, and yet no soldier may crush a bone of that sacred body. They see that he is dead already, and they break not his legs.

As yet you have only seen one of the prophecies fulfilled. He must be pierced as well. And what was that which came into that Roman soldier's mind when, in a hasty moment, he resolved to make sure that the apparent death of Jesus was a real one? Why did he open that sacred side with his lance? He knew nothing of the prophecy; he had no dreams of Eve being taken from the side of the man, and the church from the side of Jesus. He had never heard that ancient notion of the side of Jesus being like the door of the ark, through which an entrance to safety is opened. Why, then, does he fulfill the prediction of the prophet? There was no accident or chance here. Where are there such things? The hand of the Lord is here, and we desire to praise and bless that omniscient and omnipotent Providence which thus fulfilled the word of revelation.

God hath respect unto his own word, and while he takes care that no bone of his Son shall be broken, he also secures that no text of Holy Scripture shall be broken. That our Lord's bones should remain unbroken, and yet that he should be pierced, seemed a very unlikely thing; but it was carried out. When next you meet with an unlikely promise, believe it firmly. When next you see things working contrary to the truth of God, believe God, and believe nothing else. Let God be true and every man a liar (Romans 3:4). Though men and devils should give God the lie, hold you on to what God has spoken; for heaven and earth shall pass away, but not one jot or tittle of his word shall fall to the ground (Matthew 5:18).

Note again, dear friends, concerning this fulfillment of Scripture, that it was altogether indispensable. If they had broken Christ's bones, then that word of John the Baptist, "Behold the Lamb of God" (John 1:29), had seemed to have a slur cast upon it. Men would have objected, "But the bones of the Lamb of God were not broken." It was especially commanded twice over, not only in the first ordaining of the Passover in Egypt, but in the allowance of a second to those who were defiled at the time of the first Passover (Numbers 9:12). How, then, if our Lord's bones had been broken, could we have said, "Christ our Passover is sacrificed for us," when there would have been this fatal flaw? Jesus must remain intact upon the cross, and he must also be pierced; for else that famous passage in Zechariah, which is here alluded to, "They shall look on me whom they have pierced," could not have been true of him. Both prophecies must be carried out, and they were so in a conspicuous manner. But why need I say that this fulfillment was indispensable? Beloved, the keeping of every word of God is indispensable.

It is indispensable to the truth of God that he should be true always; for if one word of his can fall to the ground, then all may fall, and his veracity is gone. If it can be demonstrated that one prophecy was a mistake, then all the rest may be mistakes. If one part of the Scripture is untrue, all may be untrue, and we have no sure ground to go upon. Faith loves not slippery places; faith seeks the sure word of prophecy, and sets her foot firmly upon certainties. Unless all the Word of God is sure, and pure "like silver refined in a furnace on the ground, purified seven times" (Psalm 12:6), then we have nothing to go upon, and are virtually left without a revelation from God. If I am to take the Bible and say, "Some of this is true, and some of it is questionable," I am no better off than if I had no Bible. A man who is at sea with a chart which is only accurate in certain places, is not much better off than if he had no chart at all. Beloved, it is indispensable to the honor of God and to our confidence in his Word, that every line of Holy Scripture should be true. It was indispensable evidently in the case now before us, and this is only one instance of a rule which is without exception.

Day 27
The Death of Christ

Yet it was the will of the Lord to crush him;
he has put him to grief;
when his soul makes an offering for guilt,
he shall see his offspring; he shall prolong his days;
the will of the Lord shall prosper in his hand. (Isaiah 53:10)

What was the reason for the Savior's suffering? We are told here, "His soul makes an offering for guilt." Christ was thus troubled, because his soul was an offering for sin. Now, I am going to be as plain as I can, while I preach over again the precious doctrine of the atonement of Christ Jesus our Lord. Christ was an offering for sin, in the sense of a substitute. God longed to save, but if such a word may be allowed, Justice tied his hands. "I must be just," said God; "that is a necessity of my nature. Stern as fate, and fast as immutability is the truth that I must be just. But then my heart desires to forgive—to pass by man's transgressions and pardon them. How can it be done?" Wisdom stepped in, and said, "It shall be done thus," and Love agreed with Wisdom. "Christ Jesus, the Son of God, shall stand in man's place, and he shall be offered upon Mount Calvary instead of man." Now, mark: When you see Christ going up the Mount of Doom, you see man going there: when you see Christ hurled upon his back, upon the wooden cross, you see the whole company of his elect there; and when you see the nails driven through his blessed hands and feet, it is the whole body of his Church who there, in their substitute, are nailed to the tree. And now the soldiers lift the cross and dash it down into the socket prepared for it. His bones are every one of them dislocated, and his body is thus torn with agonies which cannot be described. 'Tis manhood suffering there; 'tis the Church suffering there, in the substitute.

And when Christ dies, you are to look upon the death of Christ, not as his own dying merely, but as the dying of all those for whom he stood as the scapegoat and the substitute. It is true, Christ himself really died; it is equally true that he did not die for himself, but died as the substitute, in the room, the place, and the stead of all believers. When you die, you will die for yourselves; when Christ died, he died for you, if you be a believer in him. When you pass through the gates of the grave, you go there solitary and alone; you are not the representative of a body of men, but you pass through the gates of death as an individual; but remember, when Christ went through the sufferings of death, he was the representative Head of all his people. Understand, then, the sense in which Christ was made a sacrifice for sin.

But here lies the glory of this matter. It was as a substitute for sin that he did actually and literally suffer punishment for the sin of all his elect. When I say this, I am not to be understood as using any figure whatever, but as saying actually what I mean. Man, for his sin, was condemned to eternal fire; when God took Christ to be the substitute, it is true, he did not send Christ into eternal fire, but he poured upon him grief, so desperate, that it was a valid payment for even an eternity of fire. Man was condemned to live forever in hell. God did not send Christ forever into hell; but he put on Christ punishment that was equivalent for that. Although he did not give Christ to drink the actual hells of believers, yet he gave him a *quid pro quo*—something that was equivalent thereunto. He took the cup of Christ's agony, and he put in there, suffering, misery, and anguish, such as only God can imagine or dream of, that was the exact equivalent for all the suffering, all the woe, and all the eternal tortures of every one that shall at last stand in heaven, bought with the blood of Christ. And you say, "Did Christ drink it all to its dregs?" Did he suffer it all? Yes, my brethren, he took the cup, and

"At one triumphant draught of love,
He drank damnation dry."

He suffered all the horror of hell: In one pelting shower of iron wrath, it fell upon him, with hailstones bigger than a talent; and he stood until the black cloud had emptied itself completely. There was our debt, huge and immense; he paid the utmost farthing of whatever his people owed; and now there is not so much as a doit[11] or a farthing due to the justice of God in the way of punishment from any believer; and though we owe God gratitude, though we owe much to his love, we owe nothing to his justice; for Christ in that hour took all our sins, past, present, and to come, and was punished for them all there and then, that we might never be punished, because he suffered in our stead. Do you see, then, how it was that God the Father bruised him? Unless he had so done, the agonies of Christ could not have been an equivalent for our sufferings; for hell consists in the hiding of God's face

11. A doit is an old coin of the Netherlands and Dutch territories.

from sinners, and if God had not hidden his face from Christ, Christ could not—I see not how he could—have endured any suffering that could have been accepted as an equivalent for the woes and agonies of his people.

Methinks I heard someone say, "Do you mean us to understand this atonement that you have now preached as being a literal fact?" I say, most solemnly, I do. I pause once more; for I hear some timid soul say, "But, Sir, I am afraid I am not elect, and if so, Christ did not die for me." Stop, sir! Are you a sinner? Do you feel it? Has God the Holy Spirit made you feel that you are a lost sinner? Do you want salvation? If you do not want it, it is no hardship that it is not provided for you; but if you really feel that you want it, you are God's elect. If you have a desire to be saved, a desire given you of the Holy Spirit, that desire is a token for good. If you have begun believingly to pray for salvation, you have therein a sure evidence that you are saved. Christ was punished for you. And if now you can say,

> "Nothing in my hands I bring
> Simply to the cross I cling."

You may be as sure you are God's elect as you are sure of your own existence; for this is the infallible proof of election—a sense of need and a thirst after Christ.

Day 28
A Royal Funeral

So they took the body of Jesus and bound it in linen cloths with the spices, as is the burial custom of the Jews. Now in the place where he was crucified there was a garden, and in the garden a new tomb in which no one had yet been laid. So because of the Jewish day of Preparation, since the tomb was close at hand, they laid Jesus there.
John 19:40–42

We are expressly told, in Holy Scripture, that our Lord was buried. It was evidently not sufficient for us merely to be told that he died; we must also know that he was buried. Why was this? Was it not, first, that we might have a certificate of his death? We do not bury living men; and the Lord Jesus would not have been buried if the centurion had not certified that he was certainly dead. Christ's being given up for burial was Pilate's certificate that he had not merely pretended to die, but that it was a real death, and that his body had no life remaining in it. This is an essential point, for if Jesus did not die, he has made no atonement for sin. If he died not, then he rose not; and if he rose not, then your faith is vain, you are yet in your sins (1 Corinthians 15:17). The sepulcher, therefore, occupies a very important place in the story of the death of Jesus.

Again, was he not buried to fulfill a type which he had himself chosen? Like as Jonah was three days and three nights in the belly of the fish, in the heart of the sea, even so was the Son of Man to lie for that time in the bowels of the earth. The casting of the runaway prophet into the sea quieted the angry waves; the tempest fell asleep when he was given up as a victim; and Christ's being cast into the sea of death has quieted the storm of Almighty wrath; we sail today as on a sea of glass, because Christ was buried in those awful billows. He must fulfill the type of Jonah, or else he spoke not aright concerning himself when he said, "An evil and adulterous generation seeks for a sign, but no sign will be given to it except the sign of the prophet Jonah" (Matthew 12:39).

Further, was not our Lord buried to make his battle with death and his triumph over it more complete? He has conquered death; but he has also burst open the castle of death, that is the grave. In this matchless duel, he has set himself to fight, not only with death, but with death and the grave combined; and hence the paean of victory is not merely, "O death, where is thy sting?" but it is also, "O grave, where is thy victory?" (1 Corinthians 15:55 KJV). Christ's victory is altogether complete. He has led captivity captive (Ephesians 4:8), because he became a captive. He has vanquished all death's allies, as well as death itself, by going down into the grave, and rending its bars asunder.

Beside all this, did not our Lord die, and condescend to be buried, to sweeten the grave for his people? Unless the Lord should speedily come, as he may—God grant that he may!—we shall fall asleep, and these bodies of ours will be committed to the silence of the grave. We must not dare to dread the sepulcher; where Christ has been, we may safely and honorably go. As I told you, the other day, he left the fine linen to be the furniture of our last bed; he left the napkin rolled up by itself, that weeping friends might dry their tears thereon; he left, beside, the myrrh and aloes, about one hundred pounds' weight, which Nicodemus brought. I never heard that they were taken away from the tomb; Jesus left them there, and they still shed their sweet fragrance throughout the graves of all his saints. We are not going to a noisome vault, but to a perfumed chamber, hung with the fine linen sheets that encompassed the Christ, and odorous with the spices that shed their sweetness upon him. To die, is now our gain; to sleep in Jesus, is to be blessed indeed.

I may add, also, that I think our Lord was buried so that, from his tomb, he might leap to his throne. He goes to the lowest depths that thence he may rise to the loftiest heights. You, too, believer, may go as low as the grave, but you can never go any lower, and when you are at your lowest, you are then on your way to your highest. Your Lord stooped to conquer, so must you. You will have won the victory over death when you lie, stark and cold, upon your last bed. The adversary may think that he has defeated you, but it is not so; you shall then have broken loose from everything that hinders you from entering upon your highest service for your Lord, and you shall have entered that holy place where you shall see his face, and serve him day and night in his glorious temple.

It was needful, then, my brother, that there should be a new tomb in the garden close by Golgotha, and that our Lord should lie there. It is a very wonderful thing that he, whose face is the light of heaven, whose hands are sceptered with the government of the universe, and whose very feet are sandaled with the stars, should yet bear the image of death upon his pale countenance, and should lie there lifeless, to be handled by others, and to be wrapped as any other dead man might be, in fine linen and sweet spices.

I want to stop here, and say to you who anxiously ask, "What will become of me when I die? I am so very poor and needy,"—never think about that matter; you have enough to do to trust God till you die. As to what is to become of your body when you are dead, never fret about that. It is wonderful how God does take care of the very dust and ashes of his chosen, how, sometimes, they receive in death respect and honor which they never thought would have come to them, and after they have passed away, their children and their household are blessed of God for their sake. The God of the living forsakes not his saints in dying, or after death. As Ruth would cleave to Naomi, and said, "Where you die I will die, and there will I be buried" (Ruth 1:17), so, with greater faithfulness, does God cleave to his people; he will see them buried, and take care of their children after they are gone. This is his comforting promise, "Leave your fatherless children; I will keep them alive; and let your widows trust in me" (Jeremiah 49:11).

Day 29
The Stone Rolled Away

Now after the Sabbath, toward the dawn of the first day of the week, Mary Magdalene and the other Mary went to see the tomb. And behold, there was a great earthquake, for an angel of the Lord descended from heaven and came and rolled back the stone and sat on it.
Matthew 28:1–2

As the holy women went towards the sepulcher in the twilight of the morning, desirous to embalm the body of Jesus, they recollected that the huge stone at the door of the tomb would be a great impediment in their way, and they said one to another, "Who shall roll us away the stone?" To the women there were three difficulties. The stone of itself was huge; it was stamped with the seal of the law; it was guarded by the representatives of power. To mankind there were the same three difficulties. Death itself was a huge stone not to be moved by any strength known to mortals; that death was evidently sent of God as a penalty for offenses against his law; how could it therefore be averted, how removed? No answer was given to sages and kings, but the women who loved the Savior found an answer. They came to the tomb of Christ, but it was empty, for Jesus had risen. Here is the answer to the world's inquiry—there is another life; bodies will live again, for Jesus lives.

The stone rolled must evidently be regarded as the door of the sepulcher removed. Death's house was firmly secured by a huge stone; the angel removed it, and the living Christ came forth. The massive door, you will observe, was taken away from the grave—not merely opened, but unhinged, flung aside, rolled away; and henceforth death's ancient prison house is without a door. The saints shall pass in, but they shall not be shut in. They shall tarry there as in an open cavern, but there is nothing to prevent their coming forth from it in due time. Remember that our Lord was committed to the grave as a hostage. "He died for our sins." Like a debt they were imputed to him. He discharged the debt of obligation due from us to God, on the tree; he suffered to the full, the great substitutionary equivalent for our suffering, and then he was confined in the tomb as a hostage until his work should be fully accepted. That acceptance would be notified by his coming forth from durance vile;[12] and that coming forth would become our justification—He "was raised again for our justification" (Romans 4:25 KJV). If he had not fully paid the debt he would have remained in the grave. If Jesus had not made effectual, total, final atonement, he must have continued a captive.

But he had done it all. The "It is finished," which came from his own lips, was established by the verdict of Jehovah, and Jesus was set free. Mark him as he rises, not breaking prison like a felon who escapes from justice, but coming leisurely forth like one whose time of jail delivery is come; rising, it is true, by his own power, but not leaving the tomb without a sacred permit—the heavenly officer from the court of heaven is deputed to open the door to him, by rolling away the stone, and Jesus Christ, completely justified, rises to prove that all his people are,

12. *Durance vile* is an idiom connoting imprisonment or restraint by way of physical force.

in him, completely justified, and the work of salvation is forever perfect. The stone is rolled from the door of the sepulcher, as if to show that Jesus has so effectually done the work that nothing can shut us up in the grave again. Come, brethren, let us rejoice in this. In the empty tomb of Christ, we see sin forever put away; we see, therefore, death most effectually destroyed.

Brethren beloved in Christ, as we look at yonder stone, with the angel seated upon it, it rises before us as a monument of Christ's victory over death and hell, and it becomes us to remember that his victory was achieved for us, and the fruits of it are all ours. We have to fight with sin, but Christ has overcome it. We are tempted by Satan; Christ has given Satan a defeat. Courage, Christian soldiers, you are encountering a vanquished enemy; remember that the Lord's victory is a guarantee for yours. If the Head conquers, the members shall not be defeated. Let not sorrow dim your eye; let no fears trouble your spirit; you must conquer, for Christ has conquered. Awaken all your powers to the conflict, and nerve them with the hope of victory. Had you seen your Master defeated, you might expect yourself to be blown like chaff before the wind; but the power by which he overcame he lends to you. The Holy Ghost is in you; Jesus himself has promised to be with you always, even to the end of the world, and the mighty God is your refuge. You shall surely overcome through the blood of the Lamb. Set up that stone before your faith's eye this morning, and say, "Here my Master conquered hell and death, and in his name and by his strength I shall be crowned, too, when the last enemy is destroyed."

That stone was a boundary appointed. Do you not see it so? Behold it then, there it lies, and the angel sits upon it. On that side what see you? The guards affrighted, stiffened with fear, like dead men. On this side what see you? The timid trembling women, to whom the angel softly speaks, "Do not be afraid, for I know that you seek Jesus." You see, then, that stone became the boundary between the living and the dead, between the seekers and the haters, between the friends and the foes of Christ. The resurrection acts much in the same manner as the pillar which Jehovah placed between Israel and Egypt: It was darkness to Egypt, but it gave light to Israel. All was dark amidst Egypt's hosts, but all was brightness and comfort amongst Israel's tribes.

So the resurrection is a doctrine full of horror to those who know not Christ, and trust him not. What have they to gain by resurrection? Happy were they could they sleep in everlasting annihilation. What have they to gain by Christ's resurrection? Shall he come whom they have despised? Is he living whom they have hated and abhorred? Will he bid them rise, will they have to meet him as a Judge upon the throne? The very thought of this is enough to smite through the loins of kings today; but what will the fact of it be when the clarion trumpet startles all the sons of Adam from their last beds of dust! Oh, the horrors of that tremendous morning, when every sinner shall rise, and the risen Savior shall come in the clouds of heaven, and all the holy angels with him! Truly there is nothing but dismay for those who are on the evil side of that resurrection stone.

But how great the joy which the resurrection brings to those who are on the right side of that stone! How they look for his appearing with daily growing transport! How they build upon the sweet truth that they shall arise, and with these eyes their Savior see! I would have you ask yourselves, this morning, on which side you are of that boundary stone now. Have you life in Christ? Are you risen with Christ? Do you trust alone in him who rose from the dead?

Day 30
Jesus Appearing to Mary Magdalene

Now when he rose early on the first day of the week, he appeared first to Mary Magdalene, from whom he had cast out seven demons.
Mark 16:9

Jesus "appeared first to Mary Magdalene." Why? One answer might be, because he chose to do so. For in his sovereignty he may reveal himself to whomsoever he wills, and he may withhold himself from whomsoever he shall please. "I will have mercy on whom I will have mercy, and I will have compassion on whom I will have compassion" (Romans 9:15), may be a very grating truth to human ears, but it is truth for all that, and he who does not acknowledge it, scarcely puts God into his true place as sitting upon the throne and doing as he wills with his own. I should be content to know that he appeared to Mary Magdalene first and not to ask another question if I thought it ill to ask it, for "It is the Lord. Let him do what seems good to him" (1 Samuel 3:18); and if he will reveal himself first to her, let it be so; herein I see his grace and say, let his name be magnified in the sovereignty of his love.

But we may go a little into the matter, I think, and perhaps find some reasons. He revealed himself first to Mary Magdalene, a woman. Was it not most meet that a woman should first see the risen Savior? She was first in the transgression, let her be first in the justification. In yon garden she was first to work our woe; let her in that other garden be the first to see him who works our weal [well-being]. She takes the apple of that bitter tree which brings us all our sorrow; let her be the first to see that mighty gardener, who has planted a tree which brings forth fruit unto everlasting life. A woman let it be, for woman was last at the cross, and last at the sepulcher; let her be earliest to return. The Marys embalmed the Savior and put him into the tomb; let one of their company be selected to be the first to see him. Sisters in Christ Jesus, there is a curse which falls more heavily on you than on others—a curse which is peculiar to you; but herein you have reason to rejoice, since "Unto you a Child is born, unto you a Son is given" (Isaiah 9:6). It is by that childbearing which brings you sorrow, that we have been delivered, even through the birth of him, the Messiah, Emmanuel, God with us, whom you are privileged first to see, because he is peculiarly yours. The seed of the woman who shall bruise the serpent's head (Genesis 3:15).

The text seems to indicate that the particular reason why he appeared to this woman first was, because out of her he had cast seven devils. Perhaps no person mentioned in the Scripture has been more singularly slandered than Mary Magdalene. It has been supposed that she was a harlot, and her name has been appended to societies which have the merciful object of endeavoring to reclaim the fallen. In that sense let me say Magdalene never was a "Magdalen."[13] She was not an unchaste woman. I think I can show you that it is quite impossible that she could have been. She was a woman of substance, and ministered to Christ's necessities (Luke 8:1–3); she was possessed of wealth and property, and spent what

13. That is, a repentant prostitute.

she had upon the Savior, and was not likely, therefore, to have been one who earned her living by the pitiful trade of her sin. Moreover, she had seven devils, and that, of itself, rendered her utterly incapable, one would think, of having been guilty of the sins of the flesh. A woman, a demoniac, mad with seven devils! Who would dream that a poor creature under so dreadful a torture as this could have been a harlot! The thing is clearly impossible to any thoughtful mind.

Nevertheless, there is this about it—and here is where the mistake first arose—the possession of a devil is typical, in the Word of God, of sin. When we want to translate the miracle into spiritual meaning we are always compelled to use the indwelling of a devil to be the metaphor, the picture of the indwelling of sin. Now as Mary Magdalene had seven devils, though she was not therefore any the greater sinner, for she could not help the devils being there, yet she was thereby the more polluted; she was sevenfold polluted, and she becomes most rightly the type of the great sinner, the representative, in fact, of the very class of sinners to whom her name has been given. She was not literally such a sinner, but she was typically so, for in her there were seven devils. Typically she stands at the head of those who are the greatest of all sinners against the law, and goodness, and grace of God, but she was not so except as a type.

Now, I think you see some reason why she should be selected as the first one to be seen by Christ, because she had been a special trophy of Christ's delivering power. In her he had won a special and signal victory over the hosts of hell; a perfect number of those evil spirits had been entrenched within her, and Christ's victorious arm had driven them all out. She should ever be regarded as a most illustrious specimen of what the great Savior can achieve. In this sense, I say, she was fitted to be the first that Jesus Christ should look upon and speak to, because out of all his disciples who were daily with him, I know not of one who had experienced such a cure as that which had fallen to her lot.

Let us learn from this, that the greatness of our sin before conversion should never make us think that we may not be specially favored with the very highest grade of fellowship. If you come to Christ, if the seven devils are cast out of you, all these things shall never be mentioned against thee; but you shall stand on a par with those, who were preserved by providence and restraining grace from going into gross sins. Oh! though you have been black and vile, he can make you so white and fair that he will not blush to treat you as the man in the parable did his little ewe lamb (2 Samuel 12:1–4). You shall drink of his cup and sleep in his bosom, and be very, very dear to him, sinner though you have been. This seems to be upon the very surface of the text, that Mary Magdalene was selected to be the first to see the Savior because she was a woman—a woman out of whom seven devils had been cast—a type of a great sinner.

Day 31
A Visit to the Tomb

He is not here, for he has risen, as he said.
Come, see the place where he lay.
Matthew 28:6

Jesus Christ has really risen from the dead. Beyond a doubt it can be shown that there is as much evidence for the resurrection of Christ as for any fact in history. There is, probably, no fact in history which is so fully proven and corroborated as the fact that Jesus of Nazareth, who was nailed to the cross, and died, and was buried, did rise again. As we believe the histories of Julius Caesar—as we accept the statements of Tacitus—we are bound on the same grounds, even as historical documents, to accept the testimony of Matthew, and Mark, and Luke, and John, and of those persons who were eyewitnesses of his death, and who saw him after he had risen from the dead. That Jesus Christ rose from the dead is not an allegory and a symbol, but it is a reality. There he lay dead, friend or foe to witness—a corpse fit to be committed to the grave. Handle him, and see. It is the very Christ you knew in life. It is the very same. Look into those eyes. Were there ever such eyes in any other human form? Behold him!

Now, let it be known and understood that our faith is that those very limbs that lay stiff and cold in death became warm with life again—that the very body, with its bones and blood and flesh, which lay there, became again instinct with life, and came forth into a glorious existence. Those hands broke the piece of honeycomb and the fish in the presence of the disciples; and those lips partook thereof; and he held out those wounds and said, "Put your finger here, and see my hands;" and he bared his side, the selfsame side, and said, "put out your hand, and place it in my side. Do not disbelieve, but believe" (John 20:27). He was no phantom, no spectra. As he himself said, "A spirit does not have flesh and bones as you see that I have" (Luke 24:39). He was real man, as much after the resurrection as he had been before; and he is real man in glory now, even as he was when here below. He has gone up: The cloud has received him out of our sight.

The selfsame Christ who said unto Peter, "Do you love me?" (John 21:15–17)—the selfsame Jesus who said to all his disciples, "Come and have breakfast" (John 21:12)—a real man has really risen from a real death into a real life. Now, we always want to have that doctrine stated to us plainly, for though we believe it we do not always realize it; and even if we have realized it, it is good to hear it again, so as to let our minds be confirmed about it. The resurrection is as literal a fact as any other fact stated in history, and is so to be believed among us.

"He is not here, for he has risen."

The apostle, in the first epistle to the Corinthians, makes the whole argument for the resurrection of the body hinge upon this one question—did Christ rise from the dead (1 Corinthians 15)? If he did, then all his people must rise with him. He was a representative man, and as the Lord the Savior rose, so all his followers must. Settle the question that Christ rose, and you have settled the question that all who are in him, and conformed to his image, must rise too.

As for ourselves, it is certain that we believers in Jesus, if we shall die and be put into the grave, will be fed upon by the worms—will go back to mother earth and molder. For my part, I would never wrap the body in lead, or do it up in any way that would keep it from melting back speedily to the earth from which it came. It seems fittest and holiest to let it speedily molder back to its native dust. But here is the appointed issue. No matter what becomes of that dust, and through what transitions it may pass. It is true the roots of trees may drink up this form: It is true it may turn to grass and flowers to be fed upon by beasts; the winds may waft it thousands of miles away atom from atom; bone may be scattered from its bone; but, as surely, as the Savior rose, we shall rise too. We say not that each actual particle of this flesh shall rise; it is not necessary for the identity of the body that it should be so; but still the body shall be identical, and the selfsame body that is sown in the earth shall rise again from the earth, in a beauty and a glory of which we know but little as yet—be assured of it.

That body of the dear child of God to which you bade farewell some years ago, shall rise again. Those eyes that you closed—those very eyes—shall see the King in his beauty in the land that is very far off. Those ears that could not hear you when you spoke the last tender word—those ears shall hear the eternal melodies. That heart that grew stone cold and still, when death laid his cold hand upon the bosom, shall beat again with newness of life, and leap with joy amidst the festivities of the home-bringing, when Christ the Bridegroom shall be married to his church, the bride. That selfsame body!—Was it not the temple of the Holy Ghost? Was it not redeemed with blood? Surely it shall rise at the trump of the archangel and at the voice of God! Be sure of this: be sure of it—sure for your friend and sure for yourself. And fear not death. What is it? The grave is but a bath wherein our body, like Esther, buries itself in spices to make it sweet and fresh for the embrace of the glorious King in immortality. It is but the wardrobe where we lay aside the garment for a while. It shall come forth cleansed and purified, with many a golden spangle on it which was not there before. It was a workaday dress when we put it off; it will be a Sabbath robe when we put it on, and it will be fit for Sabbath wear. We may even long for evening to undress, if there is to be such a waking and such a putting on of garments in the presence of the King.

Day 32

The First Appearance of the Risen Lord to the Eleven

As they were talking about these things, Jesus himself stood among them, and said to them, "Peace to you!" But they were startled and frightened and thought they saw a spirit. And he said to them, "Why are you troubled, and why do doubts arise in your hearts? See my hands and my feet, that it is I myself. Touch me, and see. For a spirit does not have flesh and bones as you see that I have." And when he had said this, he showed them his hands and his feet. And while they still disbelieved for joy and were marveling, he said to them, "Have you anything here to eat?" They gave him a piece of broiled fish, and he took it and ate before them.
Luke 24:36–43

This is one of the most memorable of our Lord's many visits to his disciples after he had risen from the dead. Remember, that it occurred on the same day in which our Lord had risen from the dead, and it was the close of a long day of gracious appearings. It was the summing up of a series of interviews, all of which were proofs of the Lord's resurrection.

Everything was working up to one point: the most unbelieving of them were being driven into a corner. They must doubt the truthfulness of Magdalene and the other saintly women (Luke 24:10); they must question the veracity of Simon (Luke 24:12); they must reject the two newly-arrived brethren, and charge them with telling idle tales (Luke 24:13–33), or else they must believe that Jesus was still alive, though they had seen him die upon the cross. At that moment the chief confirmation of all presented itself; "for Jesus himself stood in the midst of them." The doors were shut; but, despite every obstacle, their Lord was present in the center of the assembly. In the presence of one whose loving smile warmed their hearts, their unbelief was destined to thaw and disappear. Jesus revealed himself in all the warmth of his vitality and love, and made them understand that it was none other than his very self, and that the Scriptures had told them it should be so. They were slow of heart to believe all that the prophets had spoken concerning him, but he brought them to it by his familiar communion with them. Oh that in a like way he would put an end to all our doubts and fears!

We have often asserted, and we affirm it yet again, that no fact in history is better attested than the resurrection of Jesus Christ from the dead. The common mass of facts accepted by all men as historical are not one-tenth as certainly assured to us as this fact is. It must not be denied by any who are willing to pay the slightest respect to the testimony of their fellow men, that Jesus, who died upon the cross, and was buried in the tomb of Joseph of Arimathea, did literally rise again from the dead.

Observe, that when this person appeared in the room, the first token that it was Jesus was his speech: they were to have the evidence of hearing: he used the same speech. No sooner did he appear than he spoke. He was never dumb, and it was natural that the great Teacher and Friend should at once salute his followers, from whom he had been so painfully parted. His first accents must have called to their minds those cheering notes with which he had closed his last address. They must have recognized that charming voice. I suppose its tone and rhythm to have been rich with a music most sweet and heavenly. A perfect voice would naturally be given to a perfect man. The very sound of it would, through their ears, have charmed conviction into their minds with a glow of joy, had they not been frozen up in unbelief. "No man ever spoke like this man" (John 7:46): they might have known him by his speech alone. There were tones of voice as well as forms of language which were peculiar to Jesus of Nazareth. About the Lord there were the air and style of one who had peace himself, and loved to communicate it to others. The tone in which he spoke peace tended to create it. He was a peacemaker, and a peace-giver, and by this sign they were driven to discern their Leader.

Thus far in the narrative they had received the evidence of their ears, and that is by no means weak evidence, but now they are to have the evidence of sight; for the Savior says to them, "See my hands and my feet, that it is I myself"; "and when he had said this, he showed them his hands and his feet" (Luke 24:39–40). John says also "his side" (John 20:20), which he specially noted because he had seen the piercing of that side, and the outflow of blood and water. They were to see and identify that blessed body which had suffered death. The nail prints were visible, both in his hands which were open before them, and also in his feet which their condescending Lord deigned to expose to their deliberate gaze. There was the mark of the gash in his side; and this the Lord Jesus graciously bared to them, as afterwards he did more fully to Thomas, when he said, "Put out your hand, and place it in my side" (John 20:27).

These were the marks of the Lord Jesus, by which his identity could be verified. Beyond this there was the general contour of his countenance, and the fashion of the whole man by which they could discern him. His body, though it was now in a sense glorified, was so far veiled as to its new condition that it retained its former likeness: They might perceive that the Lord was no longer subject to the pains and infirmities of our ordinary mortality—else his wounds had not been healed so soon; but yet there remained sure marks by which they knew that it was Jesus, and no other. He looked like a lamb that had been slain (Revelation 5:6); the signs of the Son of Man were in his hands and feet and side. Their sight of the Lord was not a hasty glimpse, but a steady inspection, for John writes, "Which we have seen with our eyes, which we looked upon" (1 John 1:1). This implies a lengthened looking, and such the Lord Jesus invited his friends to take. The Savior had not assumed a phantom body; there was bone in it as well as flesh; it was to the full as substantial as ever.

Still further to confirm the faith of the disciples, and to show them that their Lord had a real body, and not the mere form of one, he gave them evidence which appealed to their common sense. He said, "'Have you anything here to eat?' They gave him a piece of a broiled fish, and some honeycomb, and he took it and ate before them." This was an exceedingly convincing proof of his unquestionable resurrection. In very deed and fact, and not in vision and phantom, the man who had died upon the cross stood among them.

Let us just think of this and rejoice. This resurrection of our Lord Jesus is a matter of certainty; for, if you spirit this away, you have done away with the gospel altogether. If he is not risen from the dead, then is our preaching vain, and your faith is also vain; you are yet in your sins

(1 Corinthians 15:17). Justification receives its seal in the resurrection of Jesus Christ from the dead; not in his appearing as a phantom, but in his very self being loosed from death, and raised to a glorious life. This is God's mark of the acceptance of the work of the great Substitute, and of the justification of all for whom his atoning work was performed.

Day 33
The Evidence of Our Lord's Wounds

Then he said to Thomas, "Put your finger here, and see my hands; and put out your hand, and place it in my side. Do not disbelieve, but believe."
John 20:27

There are times and seasons when the strong man fails, and when the firm believer has to pause a while, and say, "Is it so?" It may be that our meditation upon the text before us may be of service to those who are touched with the malady which afflicted Thomas. Thomas was permitted to put his finger into the print of the nails for the curing of his doubts. Perhaps you and I wish that we could do something like it. "Oh, if our Lord Jesus would appear to me for once, and I might thrust my hand into his side; or, if I might for once see him, or speak with him, how confirmed should I be!" No doubt that thought has arisen in the minds of many. We shall not have such proofs, my brethren, but we shall have something near akin to them.

Crave not wonders, because it is dishonoring to the sacred Word to ask for them. You believe this Bible to be an inspired volume—the Book of God. The apostle Peter calls it "the prophetic word more fully confirmed, to which you will do well to pay attention" (2 Peter 1:19). Are you not satisfied with that? When a person, in whose veracity you have the utmost confidence, bears testimony to this or that, if you straightway reply, "I would be glad of further evidence," you are slighting your friend, and casting unjust suspicion upon him. Will you cast suspicion upon the Holy Ghost, who, by this word, bears witness unto Christ? Oh, no! let us be content with his witness. Let us not wish to see, but remain satisfied to believe. If there be difficulties in believing, is it not natural there should be, when he that believes is finite, and the things to be believed are, in themselves, infinite? Let us accept the difficulties as being in themselves, in some measure, proofs of the correctness of our position, as inevitable attendants of heavenly mysteries, when they are looked at by such poor minds as ours. Let us believe the Word, and crave no signs.

Crave no signs, because it is unreasonable that we should desire more than we have already. The testimony of the Lord Jesus Christ, contained in the Word, should alone suffice us. Beside that, we have the testimony of saints and martyrs, who have gone before us, dying triumphant in the faith. We have the testimony of many still among us, who tell us that these things are so. In part, we have the testimony of our own conscience, of our own conversion, of our own after-experience, and this is convincing testimony. Let us be satisfied with it. Thomas ought to have been content with the testimony of Mary Magdalene, and the other disciples, but he was not. We ought to trust our brethren's word. Let us not be unreasonable in craving after proofs when already proofs are afforded us without stint. Jesus says, "Blessed are those who have not seen and yet have believed" (John 20:29). Thomas had his sign, and he believed; and so far so good, but he missed a blessing peculiar to those who have not seen, and yet have believed. Do not, therefore, rob yourselves of the special favor which lights on those who, with no evidence but the witness of the Spirit of

God, are prepared at once to believe in the Lord Jesus unto eternal life.

When you want comfort, crave no sign, but turn to the wounds of your Lord. You see what Thomas did. He wanted faith, and he looked for it to Jesus wounded. He says nothing about Christ's head crowned with glory. He does not say that he must see him "with a golden sash around his chest" (Revelation 1:13). Thomas, even in his unbelief, is wise; he turns to his Lord's wounds for comfort. Whenever your unbelief prevails, follow in this respect the conduct of Thomas, and turn your eyes straightway to the wounds of Jesus. These are the founts of never-failing consolation, from which, if a man once drinks, he shall forget his misery, and remember his sorrow no more.

Turn to the Lord's wounds; and if you do, what will you see? First, you will see the tokens of your Master's love. O Lord Jesus, what are these wounds in your side, and in your hands? He answers, "These I endured when suffering for you. How can I forget you? I have graven you upon the palms of my hands. How can I ever fail to remember you? On my very heart the spear has written your name." Look at Jesus, dead, buried, risen, and then say, "He loved me, and gave himself for me" (Galatians 2:20)! There is no restorative for a sinking faith like a sight of the wounded Savior. Look, soul, and live by the proofs of his death! Come and put your finger, by faith, into the print of the nails, and these wounds shall heal you of unbelief. The wounds of our Lord are the tokens of his love.

They are, again, the seals of his death, especially that wound in his side. He must have died; for "one of the soldiers pierced his side with a spear, and at once there came out blood and water. He who saw it has borne witness" (John 19:34–35). The Son of God did assuredly die. God, who made the heavens and the earth, took to himself our nature, and in one wondrous person he was both God and man; and lo! this wondrous Son of God bore sufferings unutterable, and consummated all by his death. This is our comfort, for if he died in our stead, then we shall not die for our sins; our transgression is put away, and our iniquity is pardoned. If the sacrifice had never been slain, we might despair; but since the spear-wound proves that the great Sacrifice really died, despair is slain, hope revives, and confidence rejoices.

The wounds of Jesus are the marks of identity. By these we identify his blessed person after his resurrection. The very Christ that died has risen again. There is no illusion: There could be no mistake. It is not somebody else foisted upon us in his place; but Jesus who died has left the dead, for there are the marks of the crucifixion in his hands and in his feet, and there is the spear-thrust still. It is Jesus: this same Jesus. This is a matter of great comfort to a Christian—this indisputably proven doctrine of the resurrection of our Lord. It is the keystone of the gospel arch. Take that away, or doubt it, and there remains nothing to console you. But because Jesus died and in the selfsame person rose again, and ever lives, therefore does our heart sweetly rest, believing that "through Jesus, God will bring with him those who have fallen asleep" (1 Thessalonians 4:14); and also that the whole of the work of Jesus is true, is completed, and is accepted of God.

My hearer, whenever your soul is clouded, turn to these wounds which shine like a constellation of five bright stars. Look not to your own wounds, nor to your own pains, or sins, or prayers, or tears, but remember that "with his wounds we are healed" (Isaiah 53:5). Gaze, then; intently gaze, upon your Redeemer's wounds if you would find comfort.

Day 34
My Lord and My God

Thomas answered him, "My Lord and my God!"
John 20:28

When the apostles met on the first Lord's day after Jesus had risen, Thomas was the only disciple absent out of the eleven; on the second Lord's day Thomas was there, and he was the only disciple doubting out of the eleven. How much the fact of his doubting was occasioned and helped by the fact of his former absence I cannot say; but still it looks highly probable that had he been there at the first, he would have enjoyed the same experience as the other ten, and would have been able to say as they did, "We have seen the Lord." Let us not forsake the assembling of ourselves together as the manner of some is, for we cannot tell what loss we may sustain thereby. Though our Lord may reveal himself to single individuals in solitude as he did to Mary Magdalene, yet he more usually shows himself to two or three, and he delights most of all to come into the assembly of his servants. The Lord seems most at home when, standing in the midst of his people, he says, "Peace be with you" (John 20:26). Let us not fail to meet with our fellow believers. For my part, the assemblies of God's people shall ever be dear to me.

On the second occasion Thomas is present, and he is the only one out of the eleven who is vexed with doubts. He cannot think it possible that the Lord Jesus, who was nailed to the cross, and whose side was pierced, could have really risen from the dead. Observe joyfully the

Lord's patience with him. After the plain way in which the Lord had told his disciples that he should be crucified and would rise again from the dead, they ought to have expected the resurrection; and inasmuch as they did not they were to be blamed; what shall we say of him who in addition to all this had heard the witness of his ten comrades who had actually seen the Lord? Yet there he is, the one doubter, the one sturdy questioner who has laid down most stringent requirements as to the only way in which he will be brought to believe. Will not his Lord be provoked by his obstinacy? See how patient Jesus is! If Thomas will not be convinced except by what I must call the most gross and materialistic evidence, he will give him such evidence; if he must put his finger into the print of the nails, he shall put his finger there, if he must thrust his hand into his side, he shall be permitted to take that liberty. Oh, see how Jesus condescends to the weaknesses and even to the follies of his people!

Our Lord had special reasons for turning as he did to Thomas that day, and for taking so much trouble to bring Thomas out of his unbelieving condition. The reason must have been, surely, first, that he desired to make of Thomas a most convincing witness to the reality of his resurrection. In Thomas we have a man who was specially hard to be convinced, a man who was so obstinate as to give the lie to ten of his friends with whom he had been associated for years. I am sure that such a man would give his evidence with the accent of conviction as indeed Thomas did when he cried, "My Lord and my God." We cannot have a better witness to the fact that the Lord is risen indeed than that this cool, examining, prudent, critical Thomas arrived at an absolute certainty.

Let us consider the exclamation of Thomas, "My Lord and my God." This is a most plain and hearty confession of the true and proper deity of our Lord Jesus Christ. It is much as a man could say if he wished to assert indisputably and dogmatically that Jesus is indeed God and Lord. These are terms only applicable to Jehovah. Such expressions were known to Thomas, and he as an Israelite would never have applied them to any person whom he did not believe to be God. We are sure therefore that it was the belief of Thomas that the risen Savior was Lord and God. If this had been a mistake, the Lord Jesus would have rebuked him, for he would not have allowed him to be guilty of worshipping a mere man. No good man among us would permit a person to call him God and Lord. But the perfect Jesus accepted divine homage, and therefore we are assured that it was rightly and properly given, and we do here at this moment offer him the like adoration.

This exclamation is a brief confession of faith, "My Lord and my God." Whoever will be saved, before all things, it is necessary that he be able to unite with Thomas heartily in this creed, "My Lord and my God." I do not go in for all the minute distinctions of the Athanasian Creed, but I have no doubt that it was absolutely needful at the time it was written, and that it materially helped to check the evasions and tricks of the Arians.[14] This short creed of Thomas I like much better, for it is brief, pithy, full, sententious, and it avoids those matters of detail which

14. Arianism was a fourth-century heresy that held that Jesus was created by God the Father and thus neither coeternal nor coequal with the Father.

are the quicksands of faith. Such a belief is needful; but no man can truly hold it unless he be taught by the Holy Ghost. He can say the words, but he cannot receive the spiritual truth. No man can call Jesus "Lord" but by the Holy Ghost (1 Corinthians 12:3). It is therefore a most needful and saving creed that we should cry to the Lord Jesus, "My Lord and my God." I ask you to do this now in your hearts. Renew your faith, and confess that he who died for you is your Lord and God. Socinians[15] may call Jesus what they please; to me, he is God over all, blessed forever (Romans 9:5). I know that you say, "Amen."

Further than this, do you not think that these words of Thomas were an enthusiastic profession of his allegiance to Christ? "My Lord and my God." It was as though he paid him lowliest homage, and dedicated himself there and then in the entirety of his nature to his service. To him whom he had once doubted he now submits himself, for in him he fully believes. He does as good as say, "Henceforth, O Christ, you are my Lord, and I will serve you; you are my God, and I will worship you."

Finally, I regard it as a distinct and direct act of adoration. At the feet of the manifested Savior, Thomas cries, "My Lord and my God." It sounds like a rehearsal of the eternal song which ascends before that throne where cherubim and seraphim continually do cry, "Holy, holy, holy, is the LORD of hosts" (Isaiah 6:3). It sounds like a stray note from those choral symphonies which day without night circle the throne of the Eternal. Let us in

15. Socinians were followers of a sixteenth- and seventeenth-century sect that denied the Trinity by denying the divinity of Jesus Christ.

solemn silence now present our souls before the throne, bowing in reverent adoration unto him that was, and is, and is to come, even the Lamb that was slain, who is risen, and who lives forever. "My Lord and my God." O Son of Mary, you are also Son of the Highest, and unto my heart and spirit you are my Lord and my God, and I worship you this day!

Day 35
Faith Without Sight

Jesus said to him, "Have you believed because you have seen me? Blessed are those who have not seen and yet have believed."
John 20:29

We count those people blessed indeed who lived in our Savior's day, and saw him when he dwelt here among men. And truly blessed were their eyes, for they saw, and their ears, for they heard, what kings and prophets had long desired to see and to hear, yet were not so privileged. But we who now believe in our Lord and Savior Jesus Christ, have a blessing superior to theirs, for the benediction of the text is not to those who saw and believed, but to those who "have not seen, and yet have believed."

It is a blessed thing to trust God when you cannot trace him, to believe when you cannot see. For, first, this is a sure mark of a spiritual and renewed mind. There were some who saw Christ, who nevertheless cried, "Away with him, crucify him." There were some who saw Christ, and who could not help perceiving that there was a wonderful power in him, yet they did not believe in him, and they were not saved by him. There were persons who saw Christ, and who even in some sense believed in him, yet who believed not with true saving faith. But if any of you, who have not seen him, really believe in him, this is the evidence that you are the children of God. Let me remind you of that description of the people of God which is given by Peter, in his first epistle, the first chapter, and the eighth and ninth verses: "Though you have not seen him, you love him. Though you do not now see him, you believe in him and rejoice with joy that is inexpressible and filled with glory, obtaining the outcome of your faith, the salvation of your souls." So that the people who have received the salvation of their souls are those who love the One they have never seen, and who even rejoice in him whom they do not see.

Next, this kind of man is indeed blessed because, believing when he has not seen is a proof that his heart is right towards God. I do not know any better evidence that two persons are agreed with one another, than that they fully trust each other. If I have a friend in whom I so implicitly trust that I do not want any evidence, there should be no writing between him and me; he shall not need to say that what he says is true, if he only says it, then I am certain of the truth of it; that is because my friend and I are on such good terms with one another. And when you trust God in spite of all outward appearances and surrounding circumstances, it is a comfortable proof to yourself that you are on good terms with God, that you are walking in sweet fellowship with him, and it is one of the most blessed facts in your whole history. Perhaps God is chastening you just now, and your heart is very heavy; there are many things which seem to discourage you; but, still, you can say, "Though he slay me, I will hope in him" (Job 13:15). Ah! my dear friend, you are amongst the blessed of the Lord; ay, among the very choicely blessed ones, for it is clear that there is no quarrel between you and your God. You have been reconciled to him, and you are walking with him, even though you are walking in the dark.

There is another reason why such a person is blessed, and that is, that he is having formed in him a grand character. It is a poor character that lives only on what it sees; that is the beast's character, it is quite satisfied as long as its eye can perceive the pasture. There is no great character that can ever come to a man who has no faith. The heroes among men are all men of faith; even those who are heroes concerning common matters, the heroes of patriotism, though it may not always be faith in God that they possess, yet is it faith of some sort that braces them up, and makes them superior to the doubters all around them. It is a wondrous education to a man to be compelled to trust his God—to be driven right out from paddling along the shore in his little canoe, by a big rolling wave which carries him right out to sea, and there he is taught to be a mariner who can brave the tempest, and laugh at the hurricane. We should always remain children, and have to be carried in our mother's arms, in long clothes, if we had not trials and troubles. God often hides himself in order to teach us to trust him more, and so we grow to be men, God helping us.

And, lastly, let me remind you that we are very likely coming to a time when we shall need to believe without the use of our eyes. If our Lord Jesus Christ does not soon come, some of us shall die; and if your faith depends on your sight, what will you do when your eyes are in the grave? They are going to be there; you will not be able to carry a single particle of this wonderful telescopic, microscopic, optical arrangement of yours with you to heaven. I have seen many of my dear friends die, and I know that their eyes were still in their bodies, for I looked into them, and helped to close them. They did not take them away with them; so how do they get on now that they have no eyes? I have seen their ears left behind, and laid in their coffins; and all their senses have gone, like their seeing and hearing; and if they could not believe without their senses, what would they do in the disembodied state where they now are before the throne of God? Why, they commune with Christ without the intervention of the flesh; then, do so now, beloved. Do not always be wanting to use these poor eyeballs, these dim glasses here, for they do not see much. There are angels, in this place, flying to and fro while I am preaching. I cannot see them; it is my eyes that make me blind, for I shall see them when those eyes are gone. My Lord is also here; I know he is, for he gave his promise of old that he would be, and he is sure to keep his word. But I cannot see him; that is the fault of these poor eyes of mine.

What should I do, if I could not draw near to God without my eyes and ears and hands, without touch and taste, when I am so soon to live in a world where there will be no hands, or eyes, or ears, until the resurrection morning? Then we shall get our bodies back again; but, until then, if we are to be blessed at all, it must be in the way our Lord says in the text, by faith without sight. So, brethren, if you want to enjoy great blessings, if you wish to lead a happy life, and to die a triumphant death, if you would have a glorious interregnum between death and the coming of Christ, if you would see your Master's face with acceptance in the day of his appearing, ask that this blessing may be yours, "Blessed are they that have not seen, and yet have believed."

Day 36

Do You Love Me?

When they had finished breakfast, Jesus said to Simon Peter, "Simon, son of John, do you love me more than these?" He said to him, "Yes, Lord; you know that I love you." He said to him, "Feed my lambs."
John 21:15

How very much like to Christ before his crucifixion was Christ after his resurrection! When he appeared again to his disciples, he had cast aside none of his kind manners, he had not lost a particle of interest in their welfare; he addressed them just as tenderly as before, and called them his children and his friends. Concerning their temporal condition he was mindful, for he said, "Children, have you any meat?" And he was certainly quite as watchful over their spiritual state for after he had supplied their bodies by a rich draught from the sea, with fish (which possibly he had created for the occasion), he inquires after their souls' health and prosperity, beginning with the one who might be supposed to have been in the most sickly condition, the one who had denied his Master thrice, and wept bitterly—even Simon Peter. "Simon, son of Jonas," said Jesus, "do you love me?"

Ah! dear beloved, we have very much cause for asking ourselves this question. I do not approve of the man that says, "I know I love Christ, and I never have a doubt about it;" because we often have reason to doubt ourselves, a believer's strong faith is not a strong faith in his own love to Christ—it is a strong faith in Christ's love to him. There is no faith which always believes that it loves

Christ. Strong faith has its conflicts, and a true believer will often wrestle in the very teeth of his own feelings. "Lord, if I never did love you, nevertheless, if I am not a saint, I am a sinner Lord, I still believe; help my unbelief." The disciple can believe, when he feels no love; for he can believe that Christ loves the soul; and when he has no evidence he can come to Christ without evidence, and lay hold of him, just as he is, with naked faith, and still hold fast by him. Though he see not his signs, though he walk in darkness and there be no light, still may he trust in the Lord, and stay upon his God—but to be certain at all times that we love the Lord is quite another matter; about this we have need continually to question ourselves, and most scrupulously to examine both the nature and the extent of our evidences.

Jesus asked him, in the first place, whether he loved him better than others. Simon would not say that: He had once been a little proud—more than a little—and thought he was better than the other disciples. But this time he evaded that question, he would not say that he loved better than others. Mark how Simon Peter did answer: He did not answer as to the quantity but as to the quality of his love. He would affirm that he loved Christ, but not that he loved Christ better than others. "Lord, I cannot say how much I love you; but you know all things; you know that I do love you. So far I can affirm: as to the quantity of my love, I cannot say much about it."

O sincere Christian, you can welcome your Lord's question, and answer it with holy fear and gracious confidence. Yes, you may welcome the question. Such a question was never put to Judas. The Lord loved Peter so much that he was jealous over him, or he never would have thus challenged his attachment. And in this kind he often appeals to the affections of those whom he dearly loves. The response likewise is recorded for you, "Lord, you know all things." Can you not look up, though scorned by men, though even rejected by your minister, though kept back by the deacons, and looked upon with disesteem by some—can you not look up, and say, "Lord, you know all things, you know that I love thee?" Do it not in brag and bravado; but if you can do it sincerely, be happy, bless God that he has given you a sincere love to the Savior, and ask him to increase it from a spark to a flame, and from a grain to a mountain.

"Do you love me?" Then Jesus says to us, "One of the best evidences you can give is to feed my lambs. Have I two or three little children that love and fear my name? If you want to do a deed, which shall show that you are a true lover, and not a proud pretender; go and feed them. Are there a few little ones whom I have purchased with my blood in an infant class? Do you want to do something which shall evidence that you are indeed mine? Then sit not down with the elders, dispute not in the temple; I did that myself; but go, and sit down with the young orphans, and teach them the way to the kingdom. 'Feed my lambs.'"

Nowadays, when we get the lambs, we just turn them adrift in the meadow, and there we leave them. There are more than a hundred young people in this church who positively, though they are members, ought not to be left alone; but some of our elders, if we have elders, and some who ought to be ordained elders, should make it their business to teach them further, to instruct them in the faith, and so keep them hard and fast by the truth of Jesus Christ. If we had elders, as they had in all the apostolic churches, this might in some degree be attended to (Acts 14:23). But now the hands of our deacons are full, they do much of the work of the eldership, but they cannot do any more than they are doing, for they are toiling hard already. I would that some here whom God has gifted, and who have time, would spend their afternoons in taking a class of those who live around them, of their younger brethren, asking them to their houses for prayer and pious instruction, that so the lambs of the flock may be fed. If we had some means of feeding the lambs, it would be a good way of proving to our Savior and to the world, that we really do endeavor to follow him. I hope some of my friends will take that hint; and if, in concert with me, my brethren in office will endeavor to do something in that way, I think it will be no mean proof of their love to Christ.

But, I beseech you, do something to prove your love; do not be sitting down doing nothing. Do not be folding your hands and arms, for such people perplex a minister most, and bring the most ruin on a church—such as do nothing. Do not O Christian, say that you love Christ, and yet do nothing for him. Doing is a good sign of living; and he can scarce be alive unto God that does nothing for God. We must let our works evidence the sincerity of our love to our Master.

Day 37

The Power of the Risen Savior

And Jesus came and said to them, "All authority in heaven and on earth has been given to me. Go therefore and make disciples of all nations, baptizing them in the name of the Father and of the Son and of the Holy Spirit, teaching them to observe all that I have commanded you. And behold, I am with you always, to the end of the age."
Matthew 28:18–20

Now think a moment of these words, "All power." Jesus Christ has given to him by his Father, as a consequence of his death, "all power." It is but another way of saying that the Mediator possesses omnipotence, for omnipotence is but the Latin of "all power." What mind shall conceive, what tongue shall set in order before you, the meaning of all power? We cannot grasp it; it is high, we cannot attain unto it. Such knowledge is too wonderful for us. The power of self-existence, the power of creation, the power of sustaining that which is made, the power of fashioning and destroying, the power of opening and shutting, of overthrowing or establishing, of killing and making alive, the power to pardon and to condemn, to give and to withhold, to decree and to fulfill, to be, in a word, "head over all things to the church" (Ephesians 1:22),—all this is vested in Jesus Christ our Lord. We might as well attempt to describe infinity, or map the boundless as to tell what "all power" must mean; but whatever it is, it is all given to our Lord, all lodged in those hands which once were fastened to the wood of shame, all left with that heart which was pierced with the spear, all placed as a crown upon that head which was surrounded with a coronet of thorns.

"All power in heaven" is his. Observe that! Then he has the power of God, for God is in heaven, and the power of God emanates from that central throne. Jesus, then, has divine power. Whatever Jehovah can do Jesus can do. If it were his will to speak another world into existence, we should see tonight a fresh star adorning the brow of night. Were it his will at once to fold up creation like a worn-out vesture, lo the elements would pass away, and yonder heavens would be shriveled like a scroll. The power which binds the sweet influences of the Pleiades and looses the bands of Orion is with the Nazarene; the Crucified leads forth Arcturus with his sons. Angelic bands are waiting on the wing to do the bidding of Jesus of Nazareth, and cherubim and seraphim and the four living creatures before the throne unceasingly obey him. He who was despised and rejected of men now commands the homage of all heaven, as "God over all, blessed forever."

"All power" must include—and this is a practical point to us—all the power of the Holy Ghost. In the work which lies nearest our heart the Holy Spirit is the great force. It is he that convinces men of sin, and leads them to a Savior, gives them new hearts and right spirits, and plants them in the church, and then causes them to grow and become fruitful. The power of the Holy Ghost goes forth among the sons of men according to the will of our Lord. As the anointing oil poured upon Aaron's head ran down his beard, and bedewed the skirts of his garments (Psalm 133:2), so the Spirit which has been granted to him without measure flows from him to us.

He has the residue of the Spirit, and according to his will the Holy Ghost goes forth into the church, and from the church into the world, to the accomplishment of the purposes of saving grace. All the power of the sacred Trinity, Father, Son, and Spirit, is at the command of Jesus, who is exalted far above all principality, and power, and might, and dominion, and every name that is named, not only in this world, but in that which is to come.

My soul glows as I think of what my Lord can do. If all power is given unto him in heaven and in earth, then this morning he could convert, pardon, and save every man and woman in this place; nay, he could influence the four millions of this city to cry, "What must we do to be saved?" Nor in this city only could he work, but throughout the whole earth: If it seemed good to his infinite wisdom and power he could make every sermon to be the means of conversion of all who heard it, every Bible and every copy of the Word to become the channel of salvation to all who read it, and I know not in how short a time the cry would be heard, "Alleluia! For the Lord God Omnipotent reigns" (Revelation 19:6 NKJV). Heard that cry shall be, rest assured of that. We are on the conquering side. We have with us One who is infinitely greater than all that can be against us, since "all power" is given unto him.

Brethren, we have no doubts, we entertain no fears, for every moment of time is bringing on the grand display of the power of Jesus. We preach today, and some of you despise the gospel; we bring Christ before you, and you reject him; but God will change his hand with you before long and your despisings and your rejectings will then come to an end, for that same Jesus who went from Olivet, and ascended into heaven, will so come in like manner as he was seen to go up into heaven. He will descend with matchless pomp and power, and this astonished world which saw him crucified shall see him enthroned; and in the selfsame place where men dogged his heels and persecuted him, they shall crowd around him to pay him homage, for he must reign, and put his enemies under his feet. This same earth shall be gladdened by his triumphs which once was troubled with his griefs. And more, you may be dead before the Lord shall come, and your bodies may be rotting in the tomb, but you will know that all power is his, for at the blast of his trumpet your bodies shall rise again to stand before his terrible judgment seat. You may have resisted him here, but you will be unable to oppose him then; you may despise him now, but then you must tremble before him. "Depart from me, you cursed" (Matthew 25:41), will be to you a terrible proof that he has "all power," if you will not now accept another and a sweeter proof of it by coming unto him who bids the laboring and heavy laden partake of his rest. "Kiss the Son, lest he be angry, and you perish in the way, for his wrath is quickly kindled. Blessed are all who take refuge in him" (Psalm 2:12).

Day 38

The Power of His Resurrection

That I may know him and the power of his resurrection.
Philippians 3:10

The resurrection of the Lord Jesus was in itself a marvelous display of power. To raise the dead body of our Lord from the tomb was as great a work as the creation. The Father, the Son, and the Holy Spirit, each one wrought this greatest miracle. I need not stay to quote the texts in which the resurrection of our Lord is ascribed, to the Father, who brought again from the dead that great Shepherd of the sheep (Hebrews 13:20); nor need I mention Scriptures in which the Lord is said to have been quickened by the Holy Spirit; nor those instances in which that great work is ascribed to the Lord Jesus himself; but assuredly the sacred writings represent the divine Trinity in Unity as gloriously co-operating in the raising again from the dead the person of our Lord Jesus Christ. It was, however, a special instance of our Lord's own power. He said, "Destroy this temple, and in three days I will raise it up" (John 2:19). He also said, concerning his life, "I have authority to lay it down, and I have authority to take it up again" (John 10:18). I do not know whether I can convey my own thought to you; but what strikes me very forcibly is this—no mere man going to his grave could say, "I have authority to take my life again." The departure of life leaves the man necessarily powerless: He cannot restore himself to life. Behold the sacred body of Jesus, embalmed in spices, and wrapped about with linen; it is laid within the sealed and guarded tomb; how can it come forth to life? Yet Jesus said, "I have authority to take my life again"; and he proved it true. If, in the extremity of his weakness, he had the power to rise out of the sepulcher, and come forth in newness of life, what can he not now accomplish?

Our Lord's resurrection from the dead was a proof that he was the Messiah, that he had come upon the Father's business, that he was the Son of God, and that the covenant which Jehovah had made with him was henceforth ratified and established. He was "declared to be the Son of God in power, according to the Spirit of holiness by his resurrection from the dead" (Romans 1:4). Thus said Paul at Antioch: "And we bring you the good news that what God promised to the fathers, this he has fulfilled to us their children by raising Jesus, as also it is written in the second Psalm, 'You are my Son, today I have begotten you'" (Acts 13:32–33). Nobody witnessing our Lord's resurrection could doubt his divine character, and that his mission upon earth was from the eternal God. Well did Peter and John declare that it was the Prince of Life that God had raised from the dead. Our Lord had given this for a sign unto the caviling Pharisees, that as Jonah lay in the deep till the third day, and then came forth, even so would he himself lie in the heart of the earth till the third day, and then arise from the dead. His rising proved that he was sent of God, and that the power of God was with him. Our Lord had entered into a covenant with the Father before all worlds, wherein he had on his part engaged to finish redemption and make atonement for sin. That he had done this was affirmed by his rising again from the dead; the resurrection was the attestation of the Father to the fulfillment on the part of the second Adam of his portion in the eternal covenant. His blood is the blood of the everlasting covenant, and his resurrection is the seal of it. "Christ was raised from the dead by the glory of the Father" (Romans 6:4) as the witness of the eternal God to the glory of the Son.

The resurrection of Christ casts a sidelight upon the gospel by proving its reality and literalness. There is a tendency in this generation to spirit away the truth, and in the doing thereof to lose both the truth and its spirit. In these evil days fact is turned into myth, and truth into opinion. Our Lord's resurrection is a literal fact: When he rose from the dead he was no specter, ghost, or apparition; but as he was a real man who died the cruel death of the cross, so he was a real man who rose again from the dead, bearing in his body the marks of the crucifixion. His appearance to his familiar companions was to them no dream of the night, no fevered imagination of enthusiastic minds: for he took pains to make them sure of his real presence, and that he was really among them in his proper person.

There was as much reality about the rising of our Lord as about his death and burial. There is no fiction here. This literal fact gives reality to all that comes from him and by him. Justification is no mere easing of the conscience, it is a real arraying of the soul in righteousness: Adoption into the family of God is no fancy, but brings with it true and proper sonship. The blessings of the gospel are substantial facts, and not mere theological opinions. As the resurrection of the Lord Jesus Christ from the dead was a plain visible matter of fact, so are the pardon of sin and the salvation of the soul matters of actual experience, and not the creatures of religious imagination.

Brethren, such is the evidencing power of the resurrection of Christ, that when every other argument fails your faith, you may find safe anchorage in this assured fact. The currents of doubt may bear you towards the rocks of mistrust; but when your anchor finds no other hold, it may grip the fact of the resurrection of Christ from the dead. This must be true. The witnesses are too many to have been deceived; and their patient deaths on account of their belief, proved that they were not only honest men, but good men, who valued truth more than life. We know that Jesus rose from the dead; and, whatever else we are forced to question, we have no question on that score. We may be tossed about upon the sea in reference to other statements, but we step to shore again, and find terra firma in this unquestionable, firmly-established truth: "The Lord is risen indeed." Oh, that any of you who are drifting may be brought to a resting place by this fact! If you doubt the possibility of your own pardon, this may aid you to believe, for Jesus lives.

I read the other day of one who had greatly backslidden, and grievously dishonored his Lord; but he heard a sermon upon the resurrection of Christ from the dead, and it was life to him. Though he had known and believed that truth before, yet he had never realized it vividly. After service he said to the minister, "Is it so, that our Lord Jesus has really risen from the dead, and is yet alive? Then he can save me." Just so. A living Christ can say assuredly to you, "your sins are forgiven" (Matthew 9:2). He is able now to breathe into you the life eternal. The Lord is risen indeed: In this see the evidence of his power to save to the uttermost. From this first solid stone of the resurrection, you may go, step by step, over the stream of doubt, till you land on the other side, fully assured of your salvation in Christ Jesus.

Day 39

The Wounds of Jesus

And when he had said this, he showed them his hands and his feet.
Luke 24:40

And between the throne and the four living creatures and among the elders I saw a Lamb standing, as though it had been slain.
Revelation 5:6

What was to be seen on Christ's hands and feet? We are taught that the prints of the nails were visible, and that in his side there was still the gash of the spear. For did he not say to Thomas? "Put your finger here, and see my hands; and put out your hand, and place it in my side. Do not disbelieve, but believe" (John 20:27). I wish to draw your attention to the ample fact, that our Lord Jesus Christ, when he rose again from the dead had in his body the marks of his passion. If he had pleased he could readily have removed them. He rose again from the dead, and he might have erased from his body everything which could be an indication of what he had suffered and endured before he descended into the tomb. But, no! Instead thereof, there were the pierced hands and feet, and there was the open side. Why should Christ wear these wounds in heaven and of what avail are they?

I can conceive, first, that the wounds of Christ in heaven will be a theme of eternal wonder to the angels. An old writer represents the angels as saying, "Oh, Lord of glory, what are these wounds in thy hand?" They had seen him depart from heaven, and they had gone with him as far as they might go, singing, "Glory to God in the highest, peace on earth." Some of them had watched him through his pilgrimage, for he was "seen by angels" (1 Timothy 3:16). But when he returned, I doubt not that they crowded round him, bowed before him in adoration, and then put the holy question, "What are these wounds in your hand?" At any rate they were enabled to behold for themselves in heaven the man who suffered, and they could see the wounds which were produced in his body by his sufferings; and I can readily imagine that this would cause them to lift their songs higher, would prolong their shouts of triumph, and would cause them to adore him with a rapture of wonderment, such as they had never felt before. And I doubt not that every time they look upon his hands, and behold the crucified man exalted by his Father's side, they are afresh rapt in wonder, and again they strike their harps with more joyous lingers at the thought of what he must have suffered who thus bears the sears of his hard-fought battles.

Again, Christ wears these sears in his body in heaven as his ornaments. The wounds of Christ are his glories, they are his jewels and his precious things. To the eye of the believer, Christ is never so glorious, never so passing fair, as when we can say of him, "My beloved is white and ruddy" (Song of Solomon 5:10 KJV), white with innocence, and ruddy with his own blood. He never seems so beautiful as when we can see him as the rose and the lily; as the lily, matchless purity, and as the rose, crimsoned with his own gore. We may talk of Christ in his beauty, in divers places raising the dead and stilling the tempest, but oh! there never was such a matchless Christ as he that did hang upon the cross. There I behold all his beauties, all his attributes developed, all his love drawn out, all his character expressed in letters so legible, that even my poor stammering heart can read those lines and speak them out again, as I see them written in crimson upon the bloody tree. Beloved, these are to Jesus what they are to us; they are his ornaments, his royal jewels, his fair array.

Nor are these only the ornaments of Christ; they are his trophies—the trophies of his love. Have you never seen a soldier with a gash across his forehead or in his cheek? Why every soldier will tell you the wound in battle is no disfigurement—it is his honor. "If" said he, "I received a wound when I was retreating, a wound in the back, that were to my disgrace, If I have received a wound in a victory, then it is an honorable thing to be wounded." Now, Jesus Christ has scars of honor in his flesh and glory in his eyes. He has other trophies. He has divided the spoil with the strong: He has taken the captive away from his tyrant master; he has redeemed for himself a host that no man can number, who are all the trophies of his victories: But these scars, these are the memorials of the fight, and these the trophies, too. For do you not know it was from the side of Jesus that Death sucked its death? Jesus did hang upon the cross, and Death thought to get the victory. Aye, but in its victory, it destroyed itself.

Let us think again. Jesus Christ appears in heaven as the wounded one, this shows again that he has not laid aside his priesthood. If the wounds had been removed we might have forgotten that there was a sacrifice; and, mayhap, next we might have forgotten that there was a priest. But the wounds are there; then there is a sacrifice, and there is a priest also, for he who is wounded is both himself, the sacrifice and the priest. He himself is without beginning, and his priesthood is without end. When the last ransomed soul is brought in, when there shall be no more prayers to offer, Christ shall still be a priest. Though he has no sacrifice now to slay, for he is the sacrifice himself, "once for all" (Hebrews 10:10), yet still he is a priest, and when all his people as the result of that sacrifice shall be assembled around his glorious throne, he shall still be the priest.

There is another and a terrible reason why Christ wears his wounds still. It is this: Christ is coming to judge the world. Christ has with himself today the accusers of his enemies. Every time that Christ lifts his hands to heaven, the men that hate him, or despise him, are accused. The cry is remembered, "His blood be on us and on our children" (Matthew 27:25); and the sin of casting Christ away, and rejecting him, is brought before the mind of the Most High. And when Christ shall come a second time to judge the world in righteousness, seated on the great white throne, that hand of his shall be the terror of the universe. "When they look on me, on him whom they have pierced," they shall mourn for their sins (Zechariah 12:10). They would not mourn with hopeful penitence in time, they shall mourn with sorrowful remorse throughout eternity. When the multitude are gathered together, Christ shall judge the nations, and what need he to summon accusers? His own wounds are his witnesses. Why need he to summon any to convict men of sin? His own side bears their handiwork. A crucified Christ with his wounds still open will be a terrible sight for an assembled universe.

Day 40

The Ever-Living Christ

"Fear not, I am the first and the last, and the living one. I died, and behold I am alive forevermore, and I have the keys of Death and Hades."
Revelation 1:17–18

We long, sometimes, to behold Christ in his glory. Certainly, it is one of our brightest hopes that we shall see him as he is. Every true believer can say, with Job, "I know that my Redeemer lives, and at the last he will stand upon the earth. And after my skin has been thus destroyed, yet in my flesh I shall see God, whom I shall see for myself, and my eyes shall behold, and not another" (Job 19:25–27). But, brethren, as we are now constituted, we are quite unfit for the vision of our Master's glory. It was well that, when he was on earth, he veiled himself in the form of man, for when he did uplift the veil a little, as he did on the mountain of transfiguration, the sight, though it was but a glimpse, was too much for Peter, and James, and John. They were overpowered by it, they fell asleep even upon the holy mount; and even when they were awake, they knew not what to say.

And as we now are, if we could be favored with a sight of Christ in his glory, it would be too much for us also. It was too much even for John, and we are far inferior to him; our eyes are not as clear and strong as his eyes were; yet he could not endure that wondrous vision. The gray old saint in Patmos had been familiar with his Master more years than most of us have known him; he had laid his head upon the Savior's bosom—a privilege accorded to none beside himself; he had stood at the cross, and seen the blood and water flow from that dear heart that loved him so well; and yet, though he was "that disciple whom Jesus loved," when even he had a sight of his glorified Master, he fell at his feet as dead (Revelation 1:17). The full glory of Christ is too much for us to behold while we are here on the earth, so ask not to have it yet, dear friends. By-and-by, when you are fitted for it, and Christ has prepared a place for you, his prayer shall be fulfilled in your happy experience, "Father, I desire that they also, whom you have given me, may be with me where I am, to see my glory that you have given me" (John 17:24). He might say to each one of you, "Not yet, my child, not yet may you see me as I am; your eyes are not yet fit for such a sight as that."

Observe, beloved, how the Savior comforted John when, through the excessive glory of the vision of his Lord, he swooned away, and was as one dead. First, he laid his right hand upon him; and that is where your comfort and mine must always come from—from the hand that was crucified for us. There streams from that pierced hand a wondrous power that makes the weakest strong. And if the fact of his incarnation—the truth that Christ is flesh of our flesh, and bone of our bone—should not suffice to cheer us, then he adds, as he did to John, "Fear not." And that we also may not fear, let us consider the great source of heart-cheer to every believer, as he trembles in the presence of his glorified Master, is the fact of Christ's eternal existence: "I am alive forevermore."

Here, then, you warriors of the cross, is unique leadership. Never did men before have such a leader as this one, who has proved his ardor for the accomplishment of his purpose by dying to achieve it, and who now lives to see that purpose fully accomplished. Our Master is not dead, our Leader is alive. He still rides at the head of the army of the cross, and calls us to battle for truth and right. The ungodly hear him not; but as many as believe in him still hear his clear voice ringing out the command, "Onward, hosts of God! Forward to the fight! 'Go into all the world, and preach the gospel to every creature,' until I come." We take comfort from the fact that we are led by the living Christ. When the Cid, Rodrigo Diaz, had been slain in battle, these who had been accustomed to dread his mighty sword did not for a time know that he was dead. His followers mounted the dead Cid on horseback; and the very sight of him, though it was only his corpse that they saw, made his adversaries fly before him. We set no dead Christ in the forefront of our army; it is the living Christ who marches before us, and therefore we are confident of victory, for never was host so led as by him who can say, I am "the living one. I died, and behold I am alive forevermore."

Here is a singular guarantee. He, who was dead, is now alive; then, brethren, he will carry on his work. If, when he died, he had never risen again, but had left his cause in our puny hands, it would soon have failed. But he has risen; and "he will not grow faint or be discouraged till he has established justice in the earth; and the coastlands wait for his law" (Isaiah 42:4). His kingdom shall extend to the utmost bounds of the earth; "May desert tribes bow down before him, and his enemies lick the dust" (Psalm 72:9). Be sure of this, beloved, that there is a guarantee of victory in the fact that Christ is still alive.

In these dreary times in which we live, men tell us that Christianity is a failure, that the gospel is a delusion, and I do not know what is not going to happen. Yes, yes; but there is one very important thing which they omit to mention. He lives, he lives, HE LIVES, who can never be crucified again. The Lord has set him as King upon his holy hill of Zion, and though "the kings of the earth set themselves, and the rulers take counsel together, against the LORD and against his Anointed, saying, 'Let us burst their bonds apart and cast away their cords from us.' He who sits in the heavens laughs; the LORD holds them in derision" (Psalm 2:2–4); for the Lord reigns, and he shall reign forever and ever, Hallelujah.

Acknowledgments

This is now the third volume of Spurgeon devotions I've worked on in the Old Made New series. As always, I'm grateful to the team at New Growth Press for their vision and support for creating these resources from church history. My work on these devotions flows out of my teaching and research at Midwestern Baptist Theological Seminary and the Spurgeon Library. Many thanks to Jason K. Allen and the seminary trustees for providing the resources to benefit the church. My assistants, Isaac Pang, Olivia Hansen, and the other scholars who serve at the Spurgeon Library, helped with research, compiling, and editing. My church, Wornall Road Baptist Church, has encouraged me in these volumes. My family continues to be a source of joy and blessing. I dedicate this volume to my three children, Jubilee, Ransom, and Addison. May they come to treasure Jesus Christ as their Savior! Finally, to God be the glory for the magnificent gift of his Son. May this volume strengthen the church to hold fast to the gospel of Christ crucified and risen.